# TO THE PRAISE
# *of* HIS GLORY

Other books by Lynnda Ell:

*Changing Me, Change the World: Prayers from the Psalms, Book I*

*Words of Power, Echoes of Praise: Prayers from the Psalms, Book II*

Books are available in print, digital, and audio formats.

# TO THE PRAISE
# *of* HIS GLORY

*Prayers from the Psalms, Book III*

LYNNDA ELL

WestBow
PRESS
A DIVISION OF THOMAS NELSON

WestBow Press books may be ordered through booksellers or by contacting:

WestBow Press
A Division of Thomas Nelson
1663 Liberty Drive
Bloomington, IN 47403
www.westbowpress.com
1 (866) 928-1240

ISBN: 978-1-4908-1402-5 (sc)
ISBN: 978-1-4908-1403-2 (hc)
ISBN: 978-1-4908-1401-8 (e)

Library of Congress Control Number: 2013919612

Printed in the United States of America.

WestBow Press rev. date: 11/06/2013

**Presented to:**

_____

**By:**

_____

**On:**

_____

To my sisters in Christ who attend Anna's Bible study.

Your prayers, encouragement, and review comments

helped me write the three *Prayers from the Psalms* books.

# Contents

# ACKNOWLEDGMENTS

Writing is always very personal, and writing books on eternal matters is downright scary. I write what I think I understand of God. The more I write, The greater is my understanding of my ignorance of Him! Nevertheless, I delight in sharing my experiences. I marvel as well when the Holy Spirit shapes my thoughts and words toward experiences I could never know. Writing the prayers for the 176 verses of Psalm 119 daunted me. Every day, however, God gave me fresh inspiration, and the twenty-two prayers took shape. I share this with you so you can understand my profound gratitude for the people who upheld me in prayer as I wrote this book. Thank you, prayer partners. I hope you know this is your book too.

The prayer support was critical, but no less important was my review team. They kept me from making mistakes in the usual grammatical ways. They also helped me clarify what I wanted to say and encouraged me greatly. Many thanks to Muriel Watson, Judy Hoormann, Anna Chatelaine, Brenda Tullos, Janet Torres, Ann Gregg, Wyvonne McDaniel, Vickie Williams, and Pat Russell.

Due to the generous editorial policies of Crossway publishing, complete psalms from *The Holy Bible, English Standard Version* are included with the prayers. Thank you, Crossway, for allowing me to use significant portions of the ESV Bible in these books.

My heartfelt appreciation goes to Peter Perdue and the publishing professionals at WestBow Press. It was their commitment to excellence and their patient encouragement of an emerging author that allowed these manuscripts to become books.

Most of all, I am blessed by the opportunity to share these prayers with you. Thank you for your interest in praying from the Bible. May your life bring glory to God as you praise Him in your prayers and by your life.

# FOREWORD

According to Mark D. Roberts in his *Daily Reflection* for January 12, 2013 (thehighcalling.org), neither our association nor our prayers will be neat and tidy if we have a true relationship with God. Rather, we will abandon all pretenses and tell Him our doubts and fears as well as express our faith and trust. Modeling that truth was my purpose in the first two volumes of this series, *Changing Me, Change the World* and *Words of Power, Echoes of Praise.* This final volume of *Prayers from the Psalms,* however, focuses on another dimension of our prayers, displaying God's glory as we praise Him. Regardless of our circumstances or our level of spiritual maturity, we glorify God in our prayers when we praise Him. Praise can change our attitudes and free our minds from worry and fretting. I can only repeat St. Paul's command to the church at Philippi: "Rejoice in the Lord always" (Philippians 4:4).

The photo on the front cover has special significance. For centuries, many cultures used rock cairns as physical reminders of significant events. God told Joshua to take rocks from the bed of the Jordan River and stack them on the shore after they crossed into Canaan. Many of the psalms in this book stand as "rocks of remembrance" to God's steadfast love. May you meditate on His love and praise Him.

If you are reading one of this series for the first time, it may help you to know that the format differs from most books. The psalm always appears on the left page, while the prayer for the psalm always appears on the right page; this format may be confusing when the psalm or prayer spills over to another page. You will also find blank pages reserved for recording your own prayers.

Be blessed!

Lynnda Ell
Sulphur Springs, TX

# Psalm 84

1    How lovely is your dwelling place, O Lord of hosts!

2    My soul longs, yes, faints for the courts of the Lord; my heart and flesh sing for joy to the living God.

3    Even the sparrow finds a home, and the swallow a nest for herself, where she may lay her young, at your altars, O Lord of hosts, my King and my God.

4    Blessed are those who dwell in your house, ever singing your praise!

*Selah*

5    Blessed are those whose strength is in you, in whose heart are the highways to Zion.

6    As they go through the Valley of Baca they make it a place of springs; the early rain also covers it with pools.

7    They go from strength to strength; each one appears before God in Zion.

8    O Lord God of hosts, hear my prayer; give ear, O God of Jacob!

*Selah*

9    Behold our shield, O God; look on the face of your anointed!

10   For a day in your courts is better than a thousand elsewhere. I would rather be a doorkeeper in the house of my God than dwell in the tents of wickedness.

11   For the Lord God is a sun and shield; the Lord bestows favor and honor. No good thing does he withhold from those who walk uprightly.

12   O Lord of hosts, blessed is the one who trusts in you!

# BLESSINGS BEYOND COMPARE

Lord, blessings—special blessings for people who love and obey You—flow from Your temple in heaven. You open our eyes to see the beauty of Your holiness from afar. You delight us by giving us the lyrics to wonderful songs sung by the heavenly choir. Your Word fires our imagination with descriptions of exuberant worship around Your throne. You fill our hearts with the desire to join the saints in worshipping at Your feet. With confidence, we stoop to enter the mean and lowly door of death, so that once we have passed through, we can stand erect and enter Your gates with praise and come into Your courts with thanksgiving.

Heaven is our goal; life eternal in Your presence is the prize You have set before us. Yet now, in this life, we continue on our pilgrimage, but Your Spirit maps the highways in our hearts. You provide us with the strength to fight our battles, to plant the seeds, to work in Your fields.

In this sinful, desert world, You use us to carry the water of life and to spill it upon the thirsty ground, making it a place of bubbling springs and overflowing pools. We go from strength to strength in each season of our lives until we appear before You and hear You say, "Well done, my faithful one."

All these blessings that flow forever come to us because of Jesus. Behold Him, Father; He shields us from evil and makes a way for us to stand before Your throne, clothed in His righteousness. Look on His face and see His sacrifice. Look at Him and see me, forgiven.

I would rather live a single day at peace with You than to live a thousand lifetimes in rebellion. Even if You place me at the outermost edge of Your courts, I would rather live there than anywhere else. You are the satisfaction of all I desire.

As we journey through this world You give us life, protection, usefulness, and honor. We cherish every occurrence of Your care for us. Nevertheless, we yearn for the day when we shall stand before You in heaven. The smog of this sinful world often hides Your glory. In heaven, we will see Your brilliance in its fullness, not like the flickering light of a single candle. No, we will see glory brighter than the shining of the brightest star.

Oh, that will be glorious and blessing beyond compare.

# Psalm 85

---

1   Lord, you were favorable to your land; you restored the fortunes of Jacob.

2   You forgave the iniquity of your people; you covered all their sin.

    *Selah*

3   You withdrew all your wrath; you turned from your hot anger.

4   Restore us again, O God of our salvation, and put away your indignation toward us!

5   Will you be angry with us forever? Will you prolong your anger to all generations?

6   Will you not revive us again, that your people may rejoice in you?

7   Show us your steadfast love, O Lord, and grant us your salvation.

8   Let me hear what God the Lord will speak, for he will speak peace to his people, to his saints; but let them not turn back to folly.

9   Surely his salvation is near to those who fear him, that glory may dwell in our land.

10  Steadfast love and faithfulness meet; righteousness and peace kiss each other.

11  Faithfulness springs up from the ground, and righteousness looks down from the sky.

12  Yes, the Lord will give what is good, and our land will yield its increase.

13  Righteousness will go before him and make his footsteps a way.

# FOLLY LIKE A RUDDERLESS SHIP

Father, across the world, You favor those You have chosen. By Your unfathomable grace, You redeem us, covering our sins with the blood of Your Son. You forgive our iniquity and withdraw Your wrath. Because of Your incredible love, we have new hearts and new lives, and Your Holy Spirit is in our souls.

Jesus, as if it were yesterday, I remember the joy, the peace, and the awe I experienced the day I accepted You as my Savior. As I focused on You, I felt Your presence. I read the Bible to learn of You, cherishing each new understanding. I talked to You about anything and everything. My days sparkled, and my nights glowed with Your glory.

As time passed, however, I lost my sense of the wonder of Your love. The events in my life distracted me. I stopped talking to You and reading the Bible. I let the pastor's sermons and the deacon's prayers substitute for the time I once spent in Your presence. Eventually, even my church attendance dwindled and became just an occasional activity.

What folly! My heedlessness has driven me into moral stupidity, like the winds driving a rudderless ship onto a reef. Anger, resentment, and bitterness are sending roots into my heart. Bleakness fogs my days, and depression nibbles away at my nights.

I hate this, Lord. I've hit the bottom; I'm looking up to You. Revive me, God. Restore the joy of my salvation. Yank out the weeds of sin that grow in my life.

I will fight to retake the ground I lost. Holy Spirit, by the power You provide, I resolve to recover my life in You, listening to Your Word and obeying it. Father, I want to be diligent, faithful, and fruitful. Thank You for renewing these desires in my heart.

Your steadfast love ignites faithfulness in my life, and Your righteousness provokes peace in my spirit. Thank You for opening my eyes to my folly. You empower me to change, not leaving me to wallow in the futility of self-improvement.

You will give me what is good, and I will accept it. As I plow the fields and tend the crops, You will provide the harvest. You will make the path, and I will walk upon it. I will abide in You.

# PSALM 86

1    Incline your ear, O Lord, and answer me, for I am poor and needy.

2    Preserve my life, for I am godly; save your servant, who trusts in you—you are my God.

3    Be gracious to me, O Lord, for to you do I cry all the day.

4    Gladden the soul of your servant, for to you, O Lord, do I lift up my soul.

5    For you, O Lord, are good and forgiving, abounding in steadfast love to all who call upon you.

6    Give ear, O Lord, to my prayer; listen to my plea for grace.

7    In the day of my trouble I call upon you, for you answer me.

8    There is none like you among the gods, O Lord, nor are there any works like yours.

9    All the nations you have made shall come and worship before you, O Lord, and shall glorify your name.

10    For you are great and do wondrous things; you alone are God.

11    Teach me your way, O Lord, that I may walk in your truth; unite my heart to fear your name.

12    I give thanks to you, O Lord my God, with my whole heart, and I will glorify your name forever.

13    For great is your steadfast love toward me; you have delivered my soul from the depths of Sheol.

14    O God, insolent men have risen up against me; a band of ruthless men seek my life, and they do not set you before them.

15    But you, O Lord, are a God merciful and gracious, slow to anger and abounding in steadfast love and faithfulness.

# Wishy-Washy Ways

---

God, I am so frustrated. Why do You put up with me? Here I am, desperately in need of Your help. My wishy-washy ways have landed me in trouble again.

You know I trust You. I spend time with You, trying to learn Your directions. Yet when it comes to obeying You, I find myself unable to move. I want to do what is right, but I don't. That leads to days filled with trouble and nights passed in sleepless regret. I plead for Your grace as I lift my eyes and humbly present my need to be rescued.

Why do decisions about simple matters panic me? Fear freezes me in indecision. Questions racing through my mind plague me. Will my choices have consequences that I fail to see? Which choice is the one I should make? How can I decide? Lord, with my wishy-washy ways, how did You manage to draw me into Your kingdom?

I need Your help because I waited too long to decide. The situation has decayed into chaos. My inaction did not honor Your Name. If I had heeded Your Spirit's prompting, these circumstances would have brought glory to Your Name. Show me Your favor and redeem this mess.

I also need help in overcoming the sinful habit of surrendering to fear when it is time to make a decision. Lord, I fear failure. I fear it so much that I'd rather do nothing than face failure by making the wrong choice. Failure becomes my idol. Nevertheless, I confess that You alone are God. Holy Spirit, unite my heart and mind in reverent fear of the Father. Give me an undivided heart that walks in the way of truth. Imprint Your ways on my mind so that each time I face a decision, I can trust You to control the outcome. One day, one decision at a time, replace my fear with a confident trust in You.

As You make me more like Jesus—who always followed where You led—I will give You thanks with my whole heart. Please, O Lord, my God, strengthen me and take away my wishy-washy ways.

**16**   Turn to me and be gracious to me; give your strength to your servant, and save the son of your maidservant.

**17**   Show me a sign of Your favor, that those who hate me may see and be put to shame because You, Lord, have helped me and comforted me.

# My Prayer

_____

_____

_____

_____

_____

_____

_____

_____

_____

_____

_____

_____

_____

_____

_____

_____

_____

_____

_____

_____

_____

_____

# Psalm 87

1    On the holy mount stands the city he founded;

2    the Lord loves the gates of Zion more than all the dwelling places of Jacob.

3    Glorious things of you are spoken, O city of God.

*Selah*

4    Among those who know me I mention Rahab and Babylon; behold, Philistia and Tyre, with Cush— "This one was born there," they say.

5    And of Zion it shall be said, "This one and that one were born in her"; for the Most High himself will establish her.

6    The Lord records as he registers the peoples, "This one was born there."

*Selah*

7    Singers and dancers alike say, "All my springs are in you."

# CITY OF PEACE

I talk to You often, Lord Jesus, about Jerusalem, the city You have chosen as Your own. I love it because You love it. I cherish it because You walked there, taught there, bled there, and died there. In Jerusalem You gained victory over death and the grave. Nevertheless, Jerusalem is only in the process of becoming the city of peace. Now it is a fuzzy caterpillar of a place, inching its way through time, chewing its way through the generations until You return and transform it.

After the great tribulation, You will establish Jerusalem as the crown of Your thousand-year kingdom. All nations will bring tribute to this capital of the world. During that time—Jerusalem's cocoon time—the city will prosper as honor and glory flow to Your throne.

When that time ends, however, we will remember today's Jerusalem as do those who only vaguely remember their childhoods. We will recall the old city of Your passion as do those who almost remember a wisp of last night's sweet dreams. When You make all things new, when You reveal the New Jerusalem, all memories of its caterpillar past will diminish in the light of its extravagant beauty.

More majestic than the mightiest mountains, Jerusalem will blaze with Your glory. With foundations of precious stones, gates of solid pearl, and streets of pure gold, the grandeur of its beauty will be absolute perfection. Like the graceful elegance of a butterfly in flight, Your breathtaking New Jerusalem will delight all who see it.

When I was born again, I became a citizen of this city. New Jerusalem is my home forevermore. As a citizen of the city of peace, I will sing and dance in absolute rapture, praising Your Name forever.

# Psalm 88

1    O Lord, God of my salvation; I cry out day and night before you.

2    Let my prayer come before you; incline your ear to my cry!

3    For my soul is full of troubles, and my life draws near to Sheol.

4    I am counted among those who go down to the pit; I am a man who has no strength,

5    like one set loose among the dead, like the slain that lie in the grave, like those whom you remember no more, for they are cut off from your hand.

6    You have put me in the depths of the pit, in the regions dark and deep.

7    Your wrath lies heavy upon me, and you overwhelm me with all your waves.

*Selah*

8    You have caused my companions to shun me; you have made me a horror to them. I am shut in so that I cannot escape;

9    my eye grows dim through sorrow. Every day I call upon you, O Lord; I spread out my hands to you.

10    Do you work wonders for the dead? Do the departed rise up to praise you?

*Selah*

11    Is your steadfast love declared in the grave, or your faithfulness in Abaddon?

12    Are your wonders known in the darkness, or your righteousness in the land of forgetfulness?

13    But I, O Lord, cry to you; in the morning my prayer comes before you.

# SOLITARY CONFINEMENT

My Lord! My Savior! What have You done to me? I would be better off dead. The lepers must have felt this way when they were driven out of their homes and forced to live in the wild places of ancient Israel. They could not go to the temple to worship You. I cannot go to church—I feel completely cut off from You.

Lepers could not touch others or be touched by loving hands. No one touches me. Even worse, I feel cut off from Your hand. Why have You dropped me in this pit? Why does Your wrath lie heavily on me? Suicidal thoughts and deep depression overwhelm me.

In Israel, the first signs of leprosy brought complete social isolation. I feel that way, shut up, unable to communicate with others. Companions shun me, writing me off as unworthy of their time. Prison bars get thicker. My body weakens day by day. I have no way of escape. Every day I lay my hopeless, agonizing existence before You.

Do You work wonders for the dead? Thought of death is my only companion. Do the departed rise up and praise You? Oh, how I yearn to rise up and praise You. Is Your steadfast love declared in the grave? I live in a grave; will You not pour out Your love on me? Are Your wonders known in the darkness? Darkness thicker than that found in the deepest cave surrounds me. Moment by moment, You *must* sustain me.

I am left with only my prayers. From the time of my awakening to the hour of my sleep, I come before You. Do not hide Your face from me and deny me Your comfort. Affliction, terrors, and dreadful assaults surround me. I feel adrift from You, the one I love most. Take pity, my Father, on Your desolate child whose close companion is darkness.

**14** O Lord, why do you cast my soul away? Why do you hide your face from me?

**15** Afflicted and close to death from my youth up, I suffer your terrors; I am helpless.

**16** Your wrath has swept over me; your dreadful assaults destroy me.

**17** They surround me like a flood all day long; they close in on me together.

**18** You have caused my beloved and my friend to shun me; my companions have become darkness.

# My Prayer

_____

_____

_____

_____

_____

_____

_____

_____

_____

_____

_____

_____

_____

_____

_____

_____

_____

_____

_____

_____

_____

_____

# Psalm 89:1–18

1    I will sing of the steadfast love of the Lord, forever; with my mouth I will make known your faithfulness to all generations.

2    For I said, "Steadfast love will be built up forever; in the heavens you will establish your faithfulness."

3    You have said, "I have made a covenant with my chosen one; I have sworn to David my servant:

4    'I will establish your offspring forever, and build your throne for all generations.'"

*Selah*

5    Let the heavens praise your wonders, O Lord, your faithfulness in the assembly of the holy ones!

6    For who in the skies can be compared to the Lord? Who among the heavenly beings is like the Lord,

7    a God greatly to be feared in the council of the holy ones, and awesome above all who are around him?

8    O Lord God of hosts, who is mighty as you are, O Lord, with your faithfulness all around you?

9    You rule the raging of the sea; when its waves rise, you still them.

10    You crushed Rahab like a carcass; you scattered your enemies with your mighty arm.

11    The heavens are yours; the earth also is yours; the world and all that is in it, you have founded them.

12    The north and the south, you have created them;

13    You have a mighty arm; strong is your hand, high your right hand.

# SING? OH, YES!

Sing? Oh, yes, how my heart sings, Lord God. United, my heart and my lips sing of Your enduring, eternally faithful love. As long as I have breath to tell it, my song and my story will proclaim Your holiness. You are God, unique. I proclaim it to my children and my children's children and to anyone else who listens.

What a love is this that includes the universe to the farthest galaxy and the faintest star. You establish Your faithfulness everywhere. From the highest heaven to the deepest hell, You reign.

By sovereign decree, You anchored Your kingdom on earth. By royal fiat, You chose Noah, Abraham, and David with whom to covenant. You proclaimed Jesus Christ to be Your Chosen One. He redeems rebellious ones and rules over creation forever.

When the holy ones in the highest heavens witness Your decrees, they praise the wonders of Your eternal grace and mercy.

Yes, I sing, echoing those who found Your mercy astonishing. You are *Qadosh*—the Holy One—like no other. Your presence fills me with awe and reverence, for You are holy and I am not.

You are Lord God of the mighty hosts. Only You, God Almighty, could keep every promise and fulfill every covenant. Even as humanity surges like the ocean tides, You control them. According to Your ancient plans, sometimes You calm the nations, while at other times, You crush them as You did Egypt. Always, You scatter Your enemies and restrain evil.

Sing? Oh, yes, I will sing of Your faithful love now and forever. For You created all heavens and earth. From the aurora borealis to the Southern Cross, the heavens sing Your praises. The majesty of splendid mountains joyously praise Your Name.

We are blessed because You rule from Your throne of righteousness and justice. We are surrounded by Your faithfulness and love. We will shout with great rejoicing, proclaiming Your Name all the day. We will celebrate Your righteousness. Your strength will be our glory. We will sing forever of Your favor. We will honor Your eternal kingship with our grateful praise.

14    Righteousness and justice are the foundation of your throne; steadfast love and faithfulness go before you.

15    Blessed are the people who know the festal shout, who walk, O Lord, in the light of your face,

16    who exult in your name all the day and in your righteousness are exalted.

17    For you are the glory of their strength; by your favor our horn is exalted.

18    For our shield belongs to the Lord, our king to the Holy One of Israel.

# My Prayer

_____

_____

_____

_____

_____

_____

_____

_____

_____

_____

_____

_____

_____

_____

_____

_____

_____

_____

_____

_____

_____

_____

# Psalm 89:19–37

---

19  Of old you spoke in a vision to your godly one, and said: "I have granted help to one who is mighty; I have exalted one chosen from the people.

20  I have found David, my servant; with my holy oil I have anointed him,

21  so that my hand shall be established with him; my arm also shall strengthen him.

22  The enemy shall not outwit him; the wicked shall not humble him.

23  I will crush his foes before him and strike down those who hate him.

24  My faithfulness and my steadfast love shall be with him, and in my name shall his horn be exalted.

25  I will set his hand on the sea and his right hand on the rivers.

26  He shall cry to me, 'You are my Father, my God, and the Rock of my salvation.'

27  And I will make him the firstborn, the highest of the kings of the earth.

28  My steadfast love I will keep for him forever, and my covenant will stand firm for him.

29  I will establish his offspring forever and his throne as the days of the heavens.

30  If his children forsake my law and do not walk according to my rules,

31  if they violate my statutes and do not keep my commandments,

32  then I will punish their transgression with the rod and their iniquity with stripes,

33  but I will not remove from him my steadfast love or be false to my faithfulness.

# THOUSANDS OF YEARS

It's been thousands of years since You chose David to lead Your people. We read Your promises and the covenant You made. We see David astonished with the breath and the scope of Your commitment: no enemies would crush him; he would be a strong, exalted king; he would experience Your salvation; and he would live in Your faithful love. You kept all those promises in David's lifetime. He passionately loved You and honored You all the days of his life.

Even as You honored David, so You have made great and glorious promises to me. Let me never forget Your promises and see them all fulfilled. Keep my heart faithful to You.

Though David would have been satisfied with those promises, You promised him even greater blessings, a dynasty of kings from his offspring. His sons and grandsons succeeded David on the throne in Jerusalem.

When those kings failed to follow You as David did, You never deserted them, never broke Your promise even as You disciplined them. Keep me ever aware of the depth of Your love, the endurance of Your faithfulness.

You fulfilled the greatest promise of them all centuries after David lived. You delivered on the ultimate promise: Jesus Christ, Son of God, Son of David, became the offspring of promise. The Son of David is King of kings and ruler of the universe forever.

As long as the sunlight nourishes the earth, as long as the moon lights a path through the night, You will continually keep Your promises to David. In Your graciousness and generosity, You allow every person who accepts Jesus as Savior and Lord to participate in the blessings of those promises, and I am gratefully one of those people.

As thousands of years become eternity, we will praise You for the depth of Your love and for Your enduring faithfulness to David and to Jesus Christ, the Son of David.

**34**   I will not violate my covenant or alter the word that went forth from my lips.

**35**   Once for all I have sworn by my holiness; I will not lie to David.

**36**   His offspring shall endure forever, his throne as long as the sun before me.

**37**   Like the moon it shall be established forever, a faithful witness in the skies.

*Selah*

# My Prayer

_____

_____

_____

_____

_____

_____

_____

_____

_____

_____

_____

_____

_____

_____

_____

_____

_____

_____

_____

_____

_____

_____

# Psalm 89:38–52

**38**  But now you have cast off and rejected; you are full of wrath against your anointed.

**39**  You have renounced the covenant with your servant; you have defiled his crown in the dust.

**40**  You have breached all his walls; you have laid his strongholds in ruins.

**41**  All who pass by plunder him; he has become the scorn of his neighbors.

**42**  You have exalted the right hand of his foes; you have made all his enemies rejoice.

**43**  You have also turned back the edge of his sword, and you have not made him stand in battle.

**44**  You have made his splendor to cease and cast his throne to the ground.

**45**  You have cut short the days of his youth; you have covered him with shame.

*Selah*

**46**  How long, O Lord? Will you hide yourself forever? How long will your wrath burn like fire?

**47**  Remember how short my time is! For what vanity you have created all the children of man!

**48**  What man can live and never see death? Who can deliver his soul from the power of Sheol?

*Selah*

**49**  Lord, where is your steadfast love of old, which by your faithfulness you swore to David?

# HUMBLE MY HEART

Father, forgive my careless attitude concerning the covenant You have made between us. You freed me from my prison of sin, shame, and despair. At the highest cost to Yourself, You bought me and adopted me into Your family. You pour out Your love, Your attention, and Your blessings on me. Why then do I fail to respond with gratitude and loving obedience? Why must I battle to focus on You and not on myself?

You are God, the Holy. Your Holy Spirit empowers me to live according to Your will. You expect me to live by Your Word. You are the Lord God, ruler of all, expecting me to obey You. I know this and proclaim You are Lord of my life, so why don't I willingly obey You? Why do I treat Your commands so lightly?

When the Israelites were in covenant with You, they remembered only Your promise to protect them but ignored the conditions You attached to Your promises. They knew You required them to worship only You, but they disregarded that. They worshipped their neighbors' idols. They treated Your covenant like a magic charm.

The Israelites never thought they would see their kingdom destroyed. They assumed that any king from David's lineage would have Your divine protection and that they could therefore live any way they desired. They ignored Your warning that breaking the covenant would bring painful consequences.

You did not allow the Israelites to dishonor Your Name without reaping those consequences. Their offense—idolatry—was great. Even after You warned them, they refused to repent. You disciplined them with the destruction of their nation.

From the account of the Israelites' discipline, I see You expect me to treat Your covenant with honor and respect. For love of You and in reverent fear, I bow my head and humble my heart. Holy Spirit, protect me from myself. My heart's desire is to attend to Your faintest whisper. Like a well-trained soldier, I want to respond instantly to Your commands. As a servant who knows her superior so well that she anticipates his requests, so do I want to serve You, my Lord.

**50**  Remember, O Lord, how your servants are mocked, and how I bear in my heart the insults of all the many nations,

**51**  with which your enemies mock, O Lord, with which they mock the footsteps of your anointed.

**52**  Blessed be the Lord forever! Amen and Amen.

My life is so short; I don't want to waste it. If I throw it away in selfish disobedience, that would be waste enough, but even more of my life will be wasted if I fail to heed Your corrections, so You must discipline me harshly. Oh Father, how ashamed I would be if my life gave Your enemies reasons to mock me for my disgraceful lifestyle. Please protect me from myself.

# Psalm 90

1    Lord, you have been our dwelling place in all generations.

2    Before the mountains were brought forth, or ever you had formed the earth and the world, from everlasting to everlasting you are God.

3    You return man to dust and say, "Return, O children of man!"

4    For a thousand years in your sight are but as yesterday when it is past, or as a watch in the night.

5    You sweep them away as with a flood; they are like a dream, like grass that is renewed in the morning:

6    in the morning it flourishes and is renewed; in the evening it fades and withers.

7    For we are brought to an end by your anger; by your wrath we are dismayed.

8    You have set our iniquities before you, our secret sins in the light of your presence.

9    For all our days pass away under your wrath; we bring our years to an end like a sigh.

10    The years of our life are seventy, or even by reason of strength eighty; yet their span is but toil and trouble; they are soon gone, and we fly away.

11    Who considers the power of your anger, and your wrath according to the fear of you?

12    So teach us to number our days that we may get a heart of wisdom.

13    Return, O Lord! How long? Have pity on your servants!

14    Satisfy us in the morning with your steadfast love, that we may rejoice and be glad all our days.

# From Everlasting

Lord, how can I think about You correctly? I have a finite body and mind. I had a beginning; You created me in my mother's womb. After a few decades, my life on earth will end. However, You *are* the Beginning and the End. Before You brought the mountains forth or made a place for them in Your universe, You lived. No time or space can measure You. Infinity is no measure of Your size, nor does eternity describe Your length of life.

My mind relates in measures of time, but You are outside of time. Our time scales are impossibly far apart. You see a thousand years as I would experience the passage of a night of sleep. From when I go to sleep until I awake, no time seems to have passed, so what is a thousand years to You?

Our greatest scale for time is the distance light travels in a year. When I view the light of the stars, I see history so distant that I have difficulty relating to it. You, however, see light-years as if they were shooting stars flashing by in an instant. So, God, how can You see me as anything other than desert grass that sprouts up after a shower and dies the same day? What is humanity that You notice me? Nevertheless, the wonder of Your love is that You take interest in every facet of my life.

Because You love me, teach me to know You truthfully and not by humanity's myths. Give me the reverential fear and respectful awe that I need to relate to You and to display Your glory. Only then can I comprehend the gulf that separates us.

By seeing You clearly, I can understand the appalling arrogance of my rebellion against You. You are righteous and just, and Your wrath against me is a righteous verdict. I deserve only punishment, yet You offer me peace through the sacrifice of Your Son, Jesus Christ.

Through Jesus, You teach me to number my days in wisdom, seeking Your will in all I do. In Jesus, You satisfy me every day with Your steadfast love. Through good times and bad, I rejoice in You. You show me Your work and display Your glory. By King Jesus, I have favor forevermore.

**15** Make us glad for as many days as you have afflicted us, and for as many years as we have seen evil.

**16** Let your work be shown to your servants, and your glorious power to their children.

**17** Let the favor of the Lord our God be upon us, and establish the work of our hands upon us; yes, establish the work of our hands!

From everlasting to everlasting, I will learn to know You better. Throughout eternity, I will discover new reasons to celebrate Your love. In infinite days, I will find new ways to display Your glory, but that will not be long enough to fully comprehend Your being, oh magnificent God.

# Psalm 91

1   He who dwells in the shelter of the Most High will abide in the shadow of the Almighty.

2   I will say to the Lord, "My refuge and my fortress, my God, in whom I trust."

3   For he will deliver you from the snare of the fowler and from the deadly pestilence.

4   He will cover you with his pinions, and under his wings you will find refuge; his faithfulness is a shield and buckler.

5   You will not fear the terror of the night, nor the arrow that flies by day,

6   nor the pestilence that stalks in darkness, nor the destruction that wastes at noonday.

7   A thousand may fall at your side, ten thousand at your right hand, but it will not come near you.

8   You will only look with your eyes and see the recompense of the wicked.

9   Because you have made the Lord your dwelling place—the Most High, who is my refuge—

10  no evil shall be allowed to befall you, no plague come near your tent.

11  For he will command his angels concerning you to guard you in all your ways.

12  On their hands they will bear you up, lest you strike your foot against a stone.

13  You will tread on the lion and the adder; the young lion and the serpent you will trample underfoot.

14  "Because he holds fast to me in love, I will deliver him; I will protect him, because he knows my name.

# THE PROMISE OF PROTECTION

Fear. Father, I see overwhelming fear in people's eyes. Thieves, terrorists, earthquakes, wildfires, floods, civil unrest, and financial uncertainty cause hearts to falter and nerves to fail. The pressure to panic has reached the critical point for many; others are approaching it.

Many who live in a state of panic—the ones who have never acknowledged You—have nowhere to turn. Your children, however, have Your great and precious promise of protection. Thank You for providing a safe place where fear cannot follow. Your Name is a strong tower. Those who trust in You, Lord Jesus, run into it and are saved.

Therefore, Lord, I bring all I am and have to shelter in Your shadow. You are my refuge and fortress. I trust You to keep me safe.

My sins may trap me, but You deliver me from them. The pestilence of rebellion calls to me, but I resist that siren's song and burrow beneath Your wings. Your faithfulness is my shield and wall, separating me from the pestilence, shielding me from every evil.

From a high point, I look over the wall. I see terror shrouding the night, enemies attacking in daylight, disease peering from every dark corner, and famine reigning over meal times. Nevertheless, I am not afraid.

I am not afraid because You protect me. Even though thousands fall around me—and I grieve for them—only my eyes and soul will experience the full impact of the catastrophe. You surround me with an angelic host to protect me from my weaknesses; they support me so I can trample on evil and tread on corrupt powers.

When trouble, trials, and tests come to me—as they will while I live on earth—I will remember Your promise of protection. I will come before Your throne with the words of Your promise on my lips:

Because I hold fast to You in love, You will deliver me. You will protect me because I know Your Name. When I call upon You, You will answer me. You will walk with me through the fire and carry me through the flood. You will rescue me and, because I am Your child, You will honor me. You will remind me how temporary and light these trials are and satisfy me with life eternal. Every day of life everlasting, You will show me Your salvation. By the certainty of Your promise and power of Your Word, I trust in You.

**15** When he calls to me, I will answer him; I will be with him in trouble; I will rescue him and honor him.

**16** With long life I will satisfy him and show him my salvation."

# My Prayer

_____

_____

_____

_____

_____

_____

_____

_____

_____

_____

_____

_____

_____

_____

_____

_____

_____

_____

_____

_____

_____

_____

_____

# Psalm 92

1    It is good to give thanks to the Lord, to sing praises to your name, O Most High;

2    to declare your steadfast love in the morning, and your faithfulness by night,

3    to the music of the lute and the harp, to the melody of the lyre.

4    For you, O Lord, have made me glad by your work; at the works of your hands I sing for joy.

5    How great are your works, O Lord! Your thoughts are very deep!

6    The stupid man cannot know; the fool cannot understand this:

7    that though the wicked sprout like grass and all evildoers flourish, they are doomed to destruction forever;

8    but you, O Lord, are on high forever.

9    For behold, your enemies, O Lord, for behold, your enemies shall perish; all evildoers shall be scattered.

10    But you have exalted my horn like that of the wild ox; you have poured over me fresh oil.

11    My eyes have seen the downfall of my enemies; my ears have heard the doom of my evil assailants.

12    The righteous flourish like the palm tree and grow like a cedar in Lebanon.

13    They are planted in the house of the Lord; they flourish in the courts of our God.

14    They still bear fruit in old age; they are ever full of sap and green,

15    to declare that the Lord is upright; he is my rock, and there is no unrighteousness in him.

# IT'S BETTER IN HERE

Good morning, Lord! It's Sunday morning. Even though spending time with You each day is a great pleasure, on Sunday, I rejoice that I can worship You with my Christian brothers and sisters. We pray together, knowing that where two or three are gathered, You are there. We study Your Word, trusting Your Spirit to speak to our hearts. We worship You with music, singing for joy at the work of Your hands. We worship You from our hearts through prayer, with our minds in study, and through our spirits with music. As my pastor says, "It's better worshipping God in church than in doing anything else anywhere else."

In their foolishness, most people find gathering to worship You a bore, a waste of time. They say, "We get along just fine without going to church. We can worship God at the beach, in the mountains, on the lake, or in my living room. We don't need God because we have everything we want." They enjoy temporary pleasures and ignore looming eternal destruction.

By Your design, we are saved by Your Son. By the power of Your Spirit, we confess Jesus Christ is Lord. By our presence in Your church and by the songs on our lips, we display to all that You are worthy to be praised.

You lift us up to share in the glory of our Lord. From the heights, we see our adversaries defeated and evildoers scattered. You have called us to be united by Your love.

Thank You, God, for the pleasure of gathering freely and openly. Each experience is a foretaste of glory divine, for heaven's worship will outshine earth's pale light. Here, we worship out of lives soiled by sinful natures. There, we will glorify You in the radiance of righteousness. In heaven, every day will be a day to gather in Your Name. Worship will always be fresh and dynamic. Eternally, we will say, "You are our just and righteous Lord."

# Psalm 93

1    The Lord reigns; he is robed in majesty; the Lord is robed; he has put on strength as his belt. Yes, the world is established; it shall never be moved.

2    Your throne is established from of old; you are from everlasting.

3    The floods have lifted up, O Lord, the floods have lifted up their voice; the floods lift up their roaring.

4    Mightier than the thunders of many waters, mightier than the waves of the sea, the Lord on high is mighty!

5    Your decrees are very trustworthy; holiness befits your house, O Lord, forevermore.

# THE LORD REIGNS!

You reign, oh Lord, seated at the right hand of God's throne in heaven. You rule the universe, dressed in the robe of majesty with Your never-failing strength wrapped like a gold sash around Your chest. Nothing is more certain than this: You—the One who created the universe—are the only one entitled to rule.

Why then does the sound of murmuring rise from the earth? That murmuring becomes a roar of insurrection as humanity rises in rebellion against You, their rightful king. In haughty rage, they violently rebel, roaring and smashing like mighty waves against the rocks.

Like the mighty ocean waves, however, they are helpless to run upon the shore any farther than You allow. You watch them with eyes of flame set in a face shining like the sun. Your patience will soon reach an end.

What uproar can be heard above Your voice? It thunders louder than all the mightiest waterfalls combined. The Word of Your mouth is a sharp, two-edged sword. Your Word brings life or it destroys. You decree peace and life to rebels who repent, but to the unrepentant, You speak eternal destruction.

Your decrees are righteous and trustworthy, for holiness is Your divine nature. You reign now and forever. Praise to God our Father, for our Lord reigns.

# PSALM 94

1    O Lord, God of vengeance, O God of vengeance, shine forth!

2    Rise up, O judge of the earth; repay to the proud what they deserve!

3    O Lord, how long shall the wicked, how long shall the wicked exult?

4    They pour out their arrogant words; all the evildoers boast.

5    They crush your people, O Lord, and afflict your heritage.

6    They kill the widow and the sojourner, and murder the fatherless;

7    and they say, "The Lord does not see; the God of Jacob does not perceive."

8    Understand, O dullest of the people! Fools, when will you be wise?

9    He who planted the ear, does he not hear? He who formed the eye, does he not see?

10   He who disciplines the nations, does he not rebuke? He who teaches man knowledge—

11   the Lord—knows the thoughts of man, that they are but a breath.

12   Blessed is the man whom you discipline, O Lord, and whom you teach out of your law,

13   to give him rest from days of trouble, until a pit is dug for the wicked.

14   For the Lord will not forsake his people; he will not abandon his heritage;

15   for justice will return to the righteous, and all the upright in heart will follow it.

16   Who rises up for me against the wicked? Who stands up for me against evildoers?

# Whitewashed with Legal Lies

Lord, God Almighty, I am dismayed by the arrogant wielding of political power by some of the world's leaders. In countries in which the rule of law has flourished for centuries, government officials cunningly change laws to protect themselves from prosecution for illegal acts. They defy the judicial systems to bring them to justice. They speak legal lies and boast that they live above the law.

You try to reach them, God. You send Your servants who speak truth to these rulers, call them to repent, and charge them to seek Your forgiveness. They treat Your servants with contempt, throw them in jail, or kill them.

These wicked rulers who use illegal laws to whitewash sins and to corrupt government find You standing in their way. They search the world, looking for others like themselves. They band together, prop each other up, and think they are invincible.

As citizens see this happening, their respect for the law dies. A callous disregard for human life arises. The strong kill widows and strangers; they murder orphans. Those too weak to kill mock Your Name and question Your existence. The lawless rulers discover they released anarchy when they destroyed the rule of law. Thank You for restraining them now from committing worse. When the hour of judgment comes, they will panic as they see their power evaporate, as they slide toward destruction.

What am I to do? Shall I agree that black is white and evil is good? Shall I side with the fools who think You who created the ear cannot hear? Could I pretend You who formed the eye cannot see? No! You not only see and hear but also know the most fleeting thoughts of us all. You discipline nations, so I know You will rebuke these arrogant rulers.

When I am afraid, Lord, You tell me to come before You. I fear I will not be strong enough to stand publicly against these corrupt rulers. Strengthen me as I search Your Word to find the end of their story. I will take courage, knowing You will never forsake me no matter how powerful these people think they are. I will rest in You when days of trouble come.

17  If the Lord had not been my help, my soul would soon have lived in the land of silence.

18  When I thought, "My foot slips," your steadfast love, O Lord, held me up.

19  When the cares of my heart are many, your consolations cheer my soul.

20  Can wicked rulers be allied with you, those who frame injustice by statute?

21  They band together against the life of the righteous and condemn the innocent to death.

22  But the Lord has become my stronghold, and my God the rock of my refuge.

23  He will bring back on them their iniquity and wipe them out for their wickedness; the Lord our God will wipe them out.

In my times of deepest fear, I will remember that Your faithfulness has always been my shield. In times of trouble—when I feel myself slipping away—Your steadfast love steadies me. When I have too many worries to number, You bring peace to my soul. Your law, not the laws of humanity, rules my life.

# Psalm 95

1   Oh come, let us sing to the Lord; let us make a joyful noise to the rock of our salvation!

2   Let us come into his presence with thanksgiving; let us make a joyful noise to him with songs of praise!

3   For the Lord is a great God, and a great King above all gods.

4   In his hand are the depths of the earth; the heights of the mountains are his also.

5   The sea is his, for he made it, and his hands formed the dry land.

6   Oh come, let us worship and bow down; let us kneel before the Lord, our Maker!

7   For he is our God, and we are the people of his pasture, and the sheep of his hand. Today, if you hear his voice,

8   do not harden your hearts, as at Meribah, as on the day at Massah in the wilderness,

9   when your fathers put me to the test and put me to the proof, though they had seen my work.

10  For forty years I loathed that generation and said, "They are a people who go astray in their heart, and they have not known my ways."

11  Therefore I swore in my wrath, "They shall not enter my rest."

# OUR ETERNAL CELEBRATION

The wonder of it! You invited me to the greatest celebration in the universe. You generously allow me to invite everyone I know. You even publish the invitation, "Come to Me, all who labor and are heavy laden and I will give you rest." (Matthew 11:28)

We lay our burdens down and rise up rejoicing. Our sins are forgiven. You replace our hearts of stone with living hearts that throb with joy at the sound of Your Name.

See my brothers run! Watch my sisters dance! We come in exuberant worship. We sing for joy to You, Lord. We clap our hands and shout, stomp our feet, and lift our arms in jubilant thanksgiving. Our bodies, minds, and spirits burst out in celebration.

As You rise before us, a deeper thrill engulfs us. You are *Qadosh*—the holy, the only God. You created time, space, and everything within. Your hand holds the depths of the earth, trembles the mountains, rocks the ocean waves, carves the seashore.

In Your holiness, we cannot stand before You. We avert our eyes from Your glorious face. As reverent awe falls upon us, we bow before You and kneel in tribute to the Lord our maker. We gratefully acknowledge that we belong to You. We are the flock under Your care. To You belongs all our love, loyalty, and obedience.

Thank You that today is the day of salvation for those who have not yet accepted Your invitation. For those whose hearts are pulled toward the cross of Jesus Christ, You have not uttered those terrible words, "They shall not enter my rest." (Hebrews 4:3) Oh Lord, delay— delay the day when repentance is no longer possible so multitudes more will participate in our eternal celebration.

# PSALM 96

1     Oh sing to the Lord a new song; sing to the Lord, all the earth!

2     Sing to the Lord, bless his name; tell of his salvation from day to day.

3     Declare his glory among the nations, his marvelous works among all the peoples!

4     For great is the Lord, and greatly to be praised; he is to be feared above all gods.

5     For all the gods of the peoples are worthless idols, but the Lord made the heavens.

6     Splendor and majesty are before him; strength and beauty are in his sanctuary.

7     Ascribe to the Lord, O families of the peoples, ascribe to the Lord glory and strength!

8     Ascribe to the Lord the glory due his name; bring an offering, and come into his courts!

9     Worship the Lord in the splendor of holiness; tremble before him, all the earth!

10     Say among the nations, "The Lord reigns! Yes, the world is established; it shall never be moved; he will judge the peoples with equity."

11     Let the heavens be glad, and let the earth rejoice; let the sea roar, and all that fills it;

12     let the field exult, and everything in it! Then shall all the trees of the forest sing for joy

13     before the Lord, for he comes, for he comes to judge the earth. He will judge the world in righteousness, and the peoples in his faithfulness.

# HEART SONG

Listen to my heart sing, God. I sing a new song—a song of thanksgiving—because Your mercies are new every morning. My heart is overflowing with exuberant praise. I want the whole earth to join me as I give honor to Your Name.

I will declare Your glory among the nations. Your marvelous works will be the topic of my conversations. Even my most eloquent expressions of praise will not adequately describe Your splendor and majesty. Nevertheless, my lack of ability will not keep me from attempting to tell everyone about Your magnificent strength, Your indescribable beauty.

Idols are described so easily; they are made from the dust with which You created us. Finding finite words to describe You—our infinite creator—is impossible. My total inadequacy leads me to cry out to You for the power to express Your greatness.

You answer my plea by sending Your Spirit. The Holy Spirit turns my simple words into dynamic truths. They become powerful expressions that touch hearts and ascend to Your throne.

As the Holy Spirit empowers me, I *can* proclaim Your majesty. I *can* display Your glory. My prayers become interwoven with the groaning of Your Spirit and the intercession of Your Son, creating a three-part harmony in a melody of prayer. The hymn becomes incense in the courts of Your heavenly temple. There, before Your throne, I worship You in the splendor of Your holiness. I tremble before You.

When I come away from Your presence, I boldly proclaim, "The Lord reigns! Today is the day of salvation." My heart rejoices in Your loving kindness towards all humanity, but I know that some will ignore You until You stop extending Your invitation. People will be unable to ignore You when You sit, judge of all times, in unbiased judgment.

Now, the earth groans as in the pain of childbirth. However, when You come to judge, when You come to destroy sin and death, the heavens will be glad and the earth will rejoice. Even the trees will sing for joy because creation will be freed from its bondage to death. Every voice will join the universe to declare "Jesus is Lord." The universe will display Your majesty and my heart will continue to sing, "Glorious is Your Name!"

# Psalm 97

1      The Lord reigns, let the earth rejoice; let the many coastlands be glad!

2      Clouds and thick darkness are all around him; righteousness and justice are the foundation of his throne.

3      Fire goes before him and burns up his adversaries all around.

4      His lightnings light up the world; the earth sees and trembles.

5      The mountains melt like wax before the Lord, before the Lord of all the earth.

6      The heavens proclaim his righteousness, and all the peoples see his glory.

7      All worshipers of images are put to shame, who make their boast in worthless idols; worship him, all you gods!

8      Zion hears and is glad, and the daughters of Judah rejoice, because of your judgments, O Lord.

9      For you, O Lord, are most high over all the earth; you are exalted far above all gods.

10      O you who love the Lord, hate evil! He preserves the lives of his saints; he delivers them from the hand of the wicked.

11      Light is sown for the righteous, and joy for the upright in heart.

12      Rejoice in the Lord, O you righteous, and give thanks to his holy name!

# The One and Only King

Lord, kings are in short supply in our world. We have presidents, prime ministers, despots, and dictators, but we have no true kings. With the lack of human examples, we have trouble understanding the ringing declaration, "The Lord reigns!" We've lost the concepts of loyalty, fealty, and covenant keeping. We've replaced those ideas with independence, inalienable rights, and the force of law. Sovereignty and obedience are foreign to us.

Nevertheless, Your Word declares, "The Lord reigns!" Our world may attempt to hide Your throne behind clouds and thick darkness, but that doesn't change the fact that You reign. We may rebel against You, but we have no authority to void Your right to reign.

Just as lightning flashes—lighting up the night—Your reign of righteousness and justice illuminates this sin-stained world. As the earth trembles when lightning strikes, so the mountains—and the hearts of all humanity—melt when You display Your sovereignty. Every idol worshipped by humanity disintegrates before Your omnipotence. The time approaches when by faith or by force, all humanity will worship You as creation's king.

As a citizen in Your kingdom, I rejoice when I hear reports that—as You do so often—You have displayed Your right to rule the earth. I proclaim by living in covenant with You that You are Lord, the Most High. I affirm that You are exalted above all creation.

As long as the clouds and thick darkness hide You from my sight, I declare Your rule by faith. I hate evil and trust You to deliver me from the hands of the wicked. I walk in the light of Your Word, taking pleasure in serving You. Always, Lord, I rejoice in Your holy, righteous rule and declare You as the one and only King. Yours is the kingdom and the power and the glory forever.

# Psalm 98

1     Oh sing to the Lord a new song, for he has done marvelous things! His right hand and his holy arm have worked salvation for him.

2     The Lord has made known his salvation; he has revealed his righteousness in the sight of the nations.

3     He has remembered his steadfast love and faithfulness to the house of Israel. All the ends of the earth have seen the salvation of our God.

4     Make a joyful noise to the Lord, all the earth; break forth into joyous song and sing praises!

5     Sing praises to the Lord with the lyre, with the lyre and the sound of melody!

6     With trumpets and the sound of the horn make a joyful noise before the King, the Lord!

7     Let the sea roar, and all that fills it; the world and those who dwell in it!

8     Let the rivers clap their hands; let the hills sing for joy together

9     before the Lord, for he comes to judge the earth. He will judge the world with righteousness, and the peoples with equity.

# Our Most Holy Hope

I sing the song of deliverance. I rejoice in new life because, my Lord Jesus, You rose from the grave. God did not forsake You in death; He raised You to life. By this, You freed us. All our lives, we had been held in slavery by our fear of death.

The morning You rose from the grave, You fulfilled Your promise to Abraham: through You, Jesus Christ—the offspring of Abraham—all the nations of the world are blessed. The decades and the centuries passed after You made that promise to Abraham. Each day of that waiting time, You were building up to this one glorious event—Your triumphant resurrection, proof of Your victory over sin and death.

As the earth turns to face the Easter sunrise, everyone whose hope for life eternal rests in You rejoices with exuberant praises. Every sinner who has been reconciled with the Father because You died in our place breaks forth in joyous song. In all humanity's languages, we sing of Your victory over Your foes. We praise the completion of Your sacrifice that changed our world forever.

Even creation, which groans under the curse of sin, rejoices that with Your resurrection, the end of the curse has begun. The earth sees the beginning of sin's end. You, who triumphed over death, will return to earth to rule and to judge the people. Earth and all the people who trust in You look forward to that marvelous day when sin will no longer cripple Your creation. New heavens and a new earth, new life and purity unmarred by sin are the promises arising from Your resurrection, our most holy hope.

# Psalm 99

1    The Lord reigns; let the peoples tremble! He sits enthroned upon the cherubim; let the earth quake!

2    The Lord is great in Zion; he is exalted over all the peoples.

3    Let them praise your great and awesome name! Holy is he!

4    The King in his might loves justice. You have established equity; you have executed justice and righteousness in Jacob.

5    Exalt the Lord our God; worship at his footstool! Holy is he!

6    Moses and Aaron were among his priests, Samuel also was among those who called upon his name. They called to the Lord, and he answered them.

7    In the pillar of the cloud he spoke to them; they kept his testimonies and the statute that he gave them.

8    O Lord our God, you answered them; you were a forgiving God to them, but an avenger of their wrongdoings.

9    Exalt the Lord our God, and worship at his holy mountain; for the Lord our God is holy!

# WHERE ARE THE WORSHIPPERS?

God, creator of us all, You reign over Your creation. The earth trembles, quaking in Your power to move the continents, but I see nobody trembling before You. Where are the people who should be humbling themselves and praising Your great and awesome Name?

Nations rush to help survivors of typhoons, earthquakes, tornados, blizzards, and tsunamis, so why will they not also rush to Your throne and confess that You are holy? Why do we raise our fists in anger or turn away in disgust? The true and noble response would be to recognize that You execute justice and to worship at Your footstool.

In each generation, You raise up people who walk with You. They are living examples who, though men and women born in sin, honor and obey You. We might recognize the difference their faithfulness makes in their lifestyle, and we might even honor them for the fruitfulness in their lives. What we so often fail to do, God, is follow them to Your throne.

Father, my heart is heavy. So many of the people who profess to follow You speak empty words and only pretend to draw near You. We speak of You hypocritically while our hearts and minds wander far from You. We know of Your holiness only as a command taught by men.

You forgive us as we confess our indifferent, callous attitude to Your holiness. Draw us with softly spoken words or with tremendous works of power, whatever it takes. Open our eyes so we can engage our hearts and minds to worship You. Instill in us an awe-filled fear of You as we experience Your glory and glimpse Your holiness. Unite us so completely by the power of Your Spirit that every day we will exalt and worship You, declaring with our lives that You, Lord God, are holy.

# Psalm 100

1    Make a joyful noise to the Lord, all the earth!

2    Serve the Lord with gladness! Come into his presence with singing!

3    Know that the Lord, he is God! It is he who made us, and we are his; we are his people, and the sheep of his pasture.

4    Enter his gates with thanksgiving, and his courts with praise! Give thanks to him; bless his name!

5    For the Lord is good; his steadfast love endures forever, and his faithfulness to all generations.

# RELEASING THE JOY

Father, our world seems to be such a grim place. When the storms of life overwhelm us, we focus on our pain and loss. Our stories, when the trauma has passed, always make much of the terror of our experience.

Lord, work in us to change our perspective. By Your power, transform our attitude. As we acknowledge the crises through which we pass, let the events become the background against which Your loving kindness is displayed. In the foreground, let us present the glory of Your guidance and protection. Instead of tales of gloom and horror, our stories will become cause for wonder and delight.

Your merciful care during the traumas of our lives leads us to shout—releasing the joy of the Lord on all the earth. As we share the miracles in our lives with those around us, we will all want to come into Your presence with singing. Our joy and rejoicing propel us to worship You in Your house. We run eagerly to the doors of the church. With reverence and thanksgiving, we sing praise to You. With joyful noise and shouts of rejoicing, we celebrate Your goodness.

In gratitude and thanksgiving, we declare You as the Lord our God. You lead us in safety as a shepherd guides his flock. We gratefully confess we are powerless to protect ourselves—the joy of the Lord is our strength.

It is right and proper that Your own children declare Your goodness. Will those who reject You rejoice in Your blessings? They won't even recognize them! No, recognition of Your steadfast love will be found in the enthusiastic responses of Your children, who will rejoice in Your faithfulness to all generations. Oh, what marvelous, magnificent, everlasting reasons we have for rocking the world with our shouts of joyful praise!

# Psalm 101

1   I will sing of steadfast love and justice; to you, O Lord, I will make music.

2   I will ponder the way that is blameless. Oh when will you come to me? I will walk with integrity of heart within my house;

3   I will not set before my eyes anything that is worthless. I hate the work of those who fall away; it shall not cling to me.

4   A perverse heart shall be far from me; I will know nothing of evil.

5   Whoever slanders his neighbor secretly I will destroy. Whoever has a haughty look and an arrogant heart I will not endure.

6   I will look with favor on the faithful in the land, that they may dwell with me; he who walks in the way that is blameless shall minister to me.

7   No one who practices deceit shall dwell in my house; no one who utters lies shall continue before my eyes.

8   Morning by morning I will destroy all the wicked in the land, cutting off all the evildoers from the city of the Lord.

# INTEGRITY OF HEART

Lord, You give me amazing reasons to rejoice. Your steadfast love and justice give me reasons to sing all the time. Even when my voice is stilled, my mind ponders the righteous way in which You lead me. Life with You now, even in this broken world, causes me to yearn for Your return as the King of all creation. When will You come again?

I want You to be pleased with me when it is time for You to return. What joy I will feel when You say, "Well done, my good and faithful servant." Yet, to hear You say those words to me, I must *be* an obedient, diligent, and faithful servant now. Your Word promises me that Your Spirit will give me the will and the ability to follow You. Therefore, I bring before You the principles on which, by Your power, I will live my life. I lay them before You today so You might seal them in my heart and mind.

I promise to walk with integrity of heart. My actions might not always be correct or appropriate, but my heart will be fixed on You. Even when I think no one else is watching, I will live to honor Your Name. Even in the privacy of my home, I will resist temptations.

I promise to carefully select my TV programs, movies, and Internet sites so worthless content and perversity will not have access to my mind. The music I listen to will honor You. I will persistently focus on the Holy Spirit's leading to keep me from evil.

Lord, I will choose my intimate friends carefully. I will avoid gossip parties, exclusive clubs, and arrogant companions. I will search for friends who faithfully follow You. I will learn from the people who live humbly before You.

People who deceive their friends and then exclaim, "It was a joke! I was only kidding," will not be invited to share the intimacy of my home. I will not take pity on those who live lives of lies. I will challenge their way by sharing Your love with them.

Every day—morning by morning—I will ask You to search my heart and mind, inspect my previous day's actions, and test the integrity of my heart. Holy Spirit, shine Your pure light within me. By Your power, I will work with You to destroy any evil I have unwittingly invited into my life, cutting it out of my heart. Daily living in Your presence, living my life as pure and as holy as only You can make it, constantly gives me new reasons to rejoice.

# Psalm 102:1–17

1    Hear my prayer, O Lord; let my cry come to you!

2    Do not hide your face from me in the day of my distress! Incline your ear to me; answer me speedily in the day when I call!

3    For my days pass away like smoke, and my bones burn like a furnace.

4    My heart is struck down like grass and has withered; I forget to eat my bread.

5    Because of my loud groaning my bones cling to my flesh.

6    I am like a desert owl of the wilderness, like an owl of the waste places;

7    I lie awake; I am like a lonely sparrow on the housetop.

8    All the day my enemies taunt me; those who deride me use my name for a curse.

9    For I eat ashes like bread and mingle tears with my drink,

10   because of your indignation and anger; for you have taken me up and thrown me down.

11   My days are like an evening shadow; I wither away like grass.

12   But you, O Lord, are enthroned forever; you are remembered throughout all generations.

13   You will arise and have pity on Zion; it is the time to favor her; the appointed time has come.

14   For your servants hold her stones dear and have pity on her dust.

15   Nations will fear the name of the Lord, and all the kings of the earth will fear your glory.

16   For the Lord builds up Zion; he appears in his glory;

17   he regards the prayer of the destitute and does not despise their prayer.

# REPAIR THE BREACH

What happened, Lord? My life collapsed.

Before it collapsed, I rejoiced in the challenges of the work You gave me and delighted in the opportunities I had to serve others in Your Name. Now I have no health, no home, no hope. My distress radiates in all directions. Won't You do something? Look at me. Listen to me. Help me!

God, I cannot endure these circumstances. The rising sun displays my despair. I say to myself, *I have to do something,* yet I lie in my bed, my thoughts repeating the same litany of woes, digging a mental rut too deep to escape. The days fly by, and I do nothing.

Do You see my physical condition? My bones ache; they burn. The pain never lets up. In the few hours I sleep, I find no rest. I have no appetite. Anything I choke down tastes like ashes. I look like a skeleton; my skin hangs off my bones.

Just as a hungry owl circles over the wilderness in search of food, I haunt my rooms seeking relief, searching for hope. I feel completely cut off. I call the time and temperature service just to hear the sound of another person's voice. At least the sound of the voice on the telephone silences the voices in my head that mock me for my helplessness.

I drink to forget, to ease my pain, but even that fails me. Instead of forgetting, I dilute my wine with tears from a broken, hopeless heart.

God, I am Your child. You allow every situation that comes into my life. Are You angry with me? Has my sin become so great that I must suffer for it? My misery is so intense; it feels like the weight of Your anger. Are You cutting my life short because of my failure to obey You?

Speak to me, God. Open my eyes to my breach of faith. Break down the barriers in my heart so I may repent and be at peace with You. Restore my health and my life. Without the touch of Your healing hand, my life quickly fades away.

Nevertheless, even in these miserable circumstances, I will not turn away from You. You are sovereign, enthroned beyond eternity. Even though the conditions and cultures of humanity wash in and out on the shores of time like the tide, every generation concedes the supremacy of Your power.

# My Prayer

_____

_____

_____

_____

_____

_____

_____

_____

_____

_____

_____

_____

_____

_____

_____

_____

_____

_____

_____

_____

_____

_____

I willingly bow before You, even in my great distress. Just as You promised to arise and restore Jerusalem, so will You arise and restore me, all in Your appointed time. Let my healing be as miraculous as the day when all nations fear Your Name and all the kings fall before Your glory. Let those who witnesses my recovery fall on their faces before You and acknowledge You have done this great thing.

Lord, what other hope do I have? I am destitute without You. Therefore, I claim Your promise. I ask You to regard my prayer in the Name of Jesus, who paid for my breach of faith on the cross. Do not despise my prayer; rather, heal me and repair my breach.

# Psalm 102:18–28

---

**18**    Let this be recorded for a generation to come, so that a people yet to be created may praise the Lord:

**19**    that he looked down from his holy height; from heaven the Lord looked at the earth,

**20**    to hear the groans of the prisoners, to set free those who were doomed to die,

**21**    that they may declare in Zion the name of the Lord, and in Jerusalem his praise,

**22**    when peoples gather together, and kingdoms, to worship the Lord.

**23**    He has broken my strength in midcourse; he has shortened my days.

**24**    "O my God," I say, "take me not away in the midst of my days—you whose years endure throughout all generations!"

**25**    Of old you laid the foundation of the earth, and the heavens are the work of your hands.

**26**    They will perish, but you will remain; they will all wear out like a garment. You will change them like a robe, and they will pass away,

**27**    but you are the same, and your years have no end.

**28**    The children of your servants shall dwell secure; their offspring shall be established before you.

# THE WORK OF YOUR HANDS

God, thank You for recording the symphony of creation in the Bible. In it, we can listen to the music of the spheres as You create everything from photons to galaxies. The intimacy of Your tender touch conducts every beautiful note.

How painful it must have been when You heard the first discordant notes of rebellion, beginning with some of Your angels and amplified by Adam and Eve. The cacophony of sin sounded by Your most noble creatures interrupts the glory of Your music.

Through all the ages, You hear the groans of humanity—prisoners of sin under the sentence of death. Your loving desire to return them to harmony with You led to Your great sacrifice. You came to earth as Jesus Christ and took that sentence on Yourself. For every person who accepts that substitution, the discordant groans change into rapturous songs of praise.

The cacophony of sin continues to rise from the earth. A day is coming, however, when the rebellious voices will be silent. All Your saints will gather in Israel, and Jerusalem will resound in joyful chorus.

Will I see that day before I die? I want to be in that choir, Lord, but You broke my strength early in life. Even if You do not cut short my life span, my days are few. Oh, my God, take me not away in the midst of my days! What are sixty or even one hundred years of my possible life span compared to Your unending life?

Shall I wait until that day to sing? No! As long as I live, let my voice, my soul, and my spirit always be part of the great symphony of Your servants on earth.

Today, I will sing the song of Alpha and Omega.

My God, You were before the beginning of the universe.
You spoke and formed the heavens.
You moved upon the deep and created the foundations of the earth.
You designed them to last for billions of years—but not forever.

# My Prayer

_____

_____

_____

_____

_____

_____

_____

_____

_____

_____

_____

_____

_____

_____

_____

_____

_____

_____

_____

_____

_____

_____

The day will come when the universe will die.
You will cast it off like a well-loved coat that has lost its usefulness.
On that last day, Your life will be no shorter than it was on the first day of creation.
You live beyond eternity—God outside of time.

I may no longer be on earth when sin ceases to mar Your symphony, but never mind. Even if I'm not there, my children of some generation in the future will see it. You show Your faithfulness to a thousand generations of those who love and obey You. No matter how long Your great patience lengthens the time until that day arrives, my offspring will surely be a part of that crescendo of praise to our God who created the universe.

# Psalm 103

1     Bless the Lord, O my soul, and all that is within me, bless his holy name!

2     Bless the Lord, O my soul, and forget not all his benefits,

3     who forgives all your iniquity, who heals all your diseases,

4     who redeems your life from the pit, who crowns you with steadfast love and mercy,

5     who satisfies you with good so that your youth is renewed like the eagle's.

6     The Lord works righteousness and justice for all who are oppressed.

7     He made known his ways to Moses, his acts to the people of Israel.

8     The Lord is merciful and gracious, slow to anger and abounding in steadfast love.

9     He will not always chide, nor will he keep his anger forever.

10    He does not deal with us according to our sins, nor repay us according to our iniquities.

11    For as high as the heavens are above the earth, so great is his steadfast love toward those who fear him;

12    as far as the east is from the west, so far does he remove our transgressions from us.

13    As a father shows compassion to his children, so the Lord shows compassion to those who fear him.

14    For he knows our frame; he remembers that we are dust.

15    As for man, his days are like grass; he flourishes like a flower of the field;

16    for the wind passes over it, and it is gone, and its place knows it no more.

# CHALLENGE

"Why do you worship God?"

*Father, You hear the challenge. Give me the words to display Your glory. Let me speak so well of You that my challenger bows in awe of Your majesty.*

"Yahweh—God of creation—is pure and holy. Because He blesses me, I live in endless hope. Without His benefits, I would have only a hopeless end.

"When my rebellious nature—the cancer of my soul—began to devour my life, God offered me the only cure for my iniquity. He showed me the sacrifice of Jesus, who died for my sin on the cross. He forgave all my iniquities and redeemed my life from hell. He crowns me with steadfast love and mercy. No matter how long I live or how old I look, God renews my youth—the strength and vitality of my soul—every day."

"How do you know God does all this?"

*Holy Spirit, tell me what to say in answer to this question.*

"Look in the Bible at the history of the children of Israel. When they were slaves in Egypt, He freed them with mighty acts of power. He taught them His laws and made an eternal contract with them to be their God. It was a covenant of love.

"For centuries, they repeatedly rebelled against Him, worshipping wooden carvings covered with gold. Still, God showed them mercy and steadfast love. Even when He punished them, it was only to bring them back to their covenant. So overwhelming was His love for them that He showed them abundant compassion—as if they were little children who knew no better. He knows we are weak."

"Life is short! Why waste time worshipping God?"

*Jesus, help me challenge this searcher to see the true issue.*

"Yes, life *is* short—like a desert flower that blooms in a sudden shower and dies in the next day's heat. But should the desert flower refuse to bloom because it lives less than a day? Neither will I refuse to anchor my hope in God. I will worship Him from my heart, with my lips, and through my actions. I will worship only Him and do everything in my power to delight Him—just like that desert flower does by blooming.

17    But the steadfast love of the Lord is from everlasting to everlasting on those who fear him, and his righteousness to children's children,

18    to those who keep his covenant and remember to do his commandments.

19    The Lord has established his throne in the heavens, and his rules over all.

20    Bless the Lord, O you his angels, you mighty ones who do his word, obeying the voice of his word!

21    Bless the Lord, all his hosts, his ministers, who do his will!

22    Bless the Lord, all his works, in all places of his dominion. Bless the Lord, O my soul!

"My life may be short, but it will never be empty. I will never look back and ask, 'Is that all there is?' God will use my life to matter for eternity."

"And then you die, so what difference does it make?"

*God, make my words become living truth planted deep in this seeking heart.*

"Death is only the end of the rehearsal. My worship on earth is a prelude for worship in heaven, where I will join angels surrounding God's throne and will be with every kind of creature who delights in obeying Him. No longer will my eyes be dim and my hearing dull. I will experience all creation worshipping Him. Only then will I be able to bless the Lord with everything that is within me.

*Father, draw this one into Your kingdom.*

"Won't you accept God's cure for Your sin, confess that you rebel against Him, and ask Jesus to save you from eternal death?

# Psalm 104:1–23

1    Bless the Lord, O my soul! O Lord my God, you are very great! You are clothed with splendor and majesty,

2    covering yourself with light as with a garment, stretching out the heavens like a tent.

3    He lays the beams of his chambers on the waters; he makes the clouds his chariot; he rides on the wings of the wind;

4    he makes his messengers winds, his ministers a flaming fire.

5    He set the earth on its foundations, so that it should never be moved.

6    You covered it with the deep as with a garment; the waters stood above the mountains.

7    At your rebuke they fled; at the sound of your thunder they took to flight.

8    The mountains rose, the valleys sank down to the place that you appointed for them.

9    You set a boundary that they may not pass, so that they might not again cover the earth.

10    You make springs gush forth in the valleys; they flow between the hills;

11    they give drink to every beast of the field; the wild donkeys quench their thirst.

12    Beside them the birds of the heavens dwell; they sing among the branches.

13    From your lofty abode you water the mountains; the earth is satisfied with the fruit of your work.

14    You cause the grass to grow for the livestock and plants for man to cultivate, that he may bring forth food from the earth

# Splendor Greater Than the Universe

Lord, the dark sky fascinates me with its myriad display of stars and its friendly moon watching over the night. The photographs taken in space of galaxies too far to see with our eyes are even more astonishing. They give me a new appreciation of Your greatness. The pictures show a universe You filled with splendor and bestowed with majesty. How much greater than the universe is the One who created it!

You clothed Yourself in light so with our limited senses we might glimpse Your being. You wove the fabric of the heavens around You, creating natural worlds for every kind of creature. Above the waters of the universe, You built the heavenly home for angels. There You set Your throne and the most sacred space of Your heavenly tabernacle—the Holy of Holies. From heaven, You rule over all creation, sending out Your servants to do Your bidding.

Within the cosmos, You ride the galactic clouds as they hurtle through space. You surf the solar winds, delighting in the exuberant power filling all space. To work within this sphere, You give Your angels the speed of light and arm them with a sun's flaming fire.

You hold this thunderous beauty and the breathtaking magnificence in Your hand and focus on the Milky Way, an insignificant galaxy far from the universe's center. You set in place a blue rock circling an unimportant sun, and You designed a perfect world.

Before the Himalayan Mountains or the Marianas Trench existed, the world was covered by water. With a word from You, mountains pushed to the clouds and valleys sank to the depths. You created the dry ground and the oceans.

The life You were creating required more than mountains and oceans, so You bubbled up fresh springs of sweet water out of the dry ground. You sent sparkling rivers splashing down the mountains. Wild beasts and thirsty birds quenched their thirst. You watered the whole land so it would become fruitful.

You created the fruit of the earth for food—grass for livestock and cultivated plants for humanity. The variety and diversity of plant life continue to amaze us. Eons after You placed them on earth, we discover plants unknown to us and find new uses for them.

15     and wine to gladden the heart of man, oil to make his face shine and bread to strengthen man's heart.

16     The trees of the Lord are watered abundantly, the cedars of Lebanon that he planted.

17     In them the birds build their nests; the stork has her home in the fir trees.

18     The high mountains are for the wild goats; the rocks are a refuge for the rock badgers.

19     He made the moon to mark the seasons; the sun knows its time for setting.

20     You make darkness, and it is night, when all the beasts of the forest creep about.

21     The young lions roar for their prey, seeking their food from God.

22     When the sun rises, they steal away and lie down in their dens.

23     Man goes out to his work and to his labor until the evening.

Just as You provided water and food for Your creatures, You also gave them homes—habitats exactly suited for their natures. From the depths of the seas to the tops of the mountains, life flourishes. You wove all the cycles of water, earth, plants, and animals into a sturdy fabric that defies attempts to destroy it.

These cycles have the seasons You ordained. Some follow the moon, others rise and fall with the sun, and a few belong to eternity. They stream in all the cycles of the universe.

Humanity flows with our own seasons, performing the work You made for us to do. Give us the wisdom to see our place in Your creation. Give us the desire and ability to obey You in all things so we will be good stewards of the world You gave us to hold. Let the earth join the rest of the universe in singing, "Great is the God of creation."

# Psalm 104:24–35

24   O Lord, how manifold are your works! In wisdom have you made them all; the earth is full of your creatures.

25   Here is the sea, great and wide, which teems with creatures innumerable, living things both small and great.

26   There go the ships, and Leviathan, which you formed to play in it.

27   These all look to you, to give them their food in due season.

28   When you give it to them, they gather it up; when you open your hand, they are filled with good things.

29   When you hide your face, they are dismayed; when you take away their breath, they die and return to their dust.

30   When you send forth your Spirit, they are created, and you renew the face of the ground.

31   May the glory of the Lord endure forever; may the Lord rejoice in his works,

32   who looks on the earth and it trembles, who touches the mountains and they smoke!

33   I will sing to the Lord as long as I live; I will sing praise to my God while I have being.

34   May my meditation be pleasing to him, for I rejoice in the Lord.

35   Let sinners be consumed from the earth, and let the wicked be no more! Bless the Lord, O my soul! Praise the Lord!

# TRUSTING THE ONE WHO CONDUCTS

Father, when I study the creatures on the earth, I delight to discover the variety of types and the uniqueness of every one.

Water covers much of the earth, and on the surface, the oceans appear empty. However, beneath the sparkling, dancing waves, innumerable life forms inhabit the world You ordained. From krill to whales, from jellyfish to flounder, You delight in displaying a wealth of sea life. Every year, we discover another species in the nooks and crannies of the sea.

Even the ways they eat is diverse. Whales eat one season of the year, while sharks never cease hunting for food. Every creature depends completely on You to give them their food at the proper time. Lord, let me learn from them that all the good food I eat comes from Your hand.

All sea life feels dismay when You hide Your face. Teach me to be just as sensitive to Your presence. They trust You to decide the time for their last breath. Give me the wisdom to cherish each breath, for at Your word, we will all die and return to dust.

Death, however, does not deplete the world of life, for Your Spirit moves on each living being and creates the next generation from them. We play our small part in protecting the animals You create. We are partners with You in renewing the earth.

Father, You keep me ever aware of the glory You display in creation. I share Your delight in Your work. Therefore, when cataclysmic events occur, remind me that You continue creating this world minute by minute. When earthquakes rock the earth and roll tsunamis on the land, remind me that You hold all earth's creatures in Your hand. When volcanoes spew fiery rocks, comfort me with the certainty that You control it all.

Let none of the changes in Your world sway me from trusting You. When my heart grieves for the suffering of Your creatures—human or animal—let me meditate on You, acknowledging that every life is Yours to direct. Even in my grief, I will rejoice that I can trust You to end each life at exactly the right moment.

# My Prayer

_____

_____

_____

_____

_____

_____

_____

_____

_____

_____

_____

_____

_____

_____

_____

_____

_____

_____

_____

_____

As long as I live, I will protect the lives You give into my care. I will work to protect Your world as I wait for the day when all those who rebel against You are gone from the earth. Then all the pains and struggles of Your creatures will cease, and all creation will rise as one and praise You, Lord, forever. Hallelujah!

# Psalm 105:1–22

1     Oh give thanks to the Lord; call upon his name; make known his deeds among the peoples!

2     Sing to him, sing praises to him; tell of all his wondrous works!

3     Glory in his holy name; let the hearts of those who seek the Lord rejoice!

4     Seek the Lord and his strength; seek his presence continually!

5     Remember the wondrous works that he has done, his miracles, and the judgments he uttered,

6     O offspring of Abraham, his servant, children of Jacob, his chosen ones!

7     He is the Lord our God; his judgments are in all the earth.

8     He remembers his covenant forever, the word that he commanded, for a thousand generations,

9     the covenant that he made with Abraham, his sworn promise to Isaac,

10     which he confirmed to Jacob as a statute, to Israel as an everlasting covenant,

11     saying, "To you I will give the land of Canaan as your portion for an inheritance."

12     When they were few in number, of little account, and sojourners in it,

13     wandering from nation to nation, from one kingdom to another people,

14     he allowed no one to oppress them; he rebuked kings on their account,

15     saying, "Touch not my anointed ones, do my prophets no harm!"

16     When he summoned a famine on the land and broke all supply of bread,

17     he had sent a man ahead of them, Joseph, who was sold as a slave.

18     His feet were hurt with fetters; his neck was put in a collar of iron;

# KEEPER OF PROMISES

Every day, I come into Your presence with a heart full of gratitude. You give me abundant, marvelous life regardless of my circumstances. Thank You for allowing me to come before You. I praise You for who You are. I sing glad songs for Your magnificent promises. I shout with rejoicing over Your great deeds.

Holy Spirit, increase my desire to be always in God's presence as I go about my daily tasks. When people ask me about my health, prompt me to tell them about Your mercy. When they speak of the weather, fill my mouth with words about Your grace. When, in response, they ask why I speak so often about You, I will relate to them the story of Abraham and the promises You made to him.

I will tell them about Abraham leaving his home in obedience to You as he started out with his small, wandering tribe of herders. You kept Your promise to protect him—even rebuking kings on his account. Three generations later, they were still a wandering tribe. Famine threatened to destroy them, but You had already sent Jacob's son Joseph to Egypt to prepare the way for the tribe's survival. Joseph suffered first as a slave and then as a convict until You elevated him to rule Egypt as the king's highest deputy.

As people hear about Your faithful care of Abraham's family through day-to-day dangers and catastrophic events, let them put their hope in You. Encourage them to draw near You when circumstances threaten.

Even as Joseph faithfully served You in slavery and in prison, show us the way to diligently obey You. Give us faith to continue our work every difficult day. Remind us that, regardless of the blackness of the night, You always care for us. You always keep Your promises.

19     until what he had said came to pass, the word of the Lord tested him.

20     The king sent and released him; the ruler of the peoples set him free;

21     he made him lord of his house and ruler of all his possessions,

22     to bind his princes at his pleasure and to teach his elders wisdom.

# My Prayer

_____

_____

_____

_____

_____

_____

_____

_____

_____

_____

_____

_____

_____

_____

_____

_____

_____

_____

_____

_____

_____

_____

_____

# Psalm 105:23–45

23     Then Israel came to Egypt; Jacob sojourned in the land of Ham.

24     And the Lord made his people very fruitful and made them stronger than their foes.

25     He turned their hearts to hate his people, to deal craftily with his servants.

26     He sent Moses, his servant, and Aaron, whom he had chosen.

27     They performed his signs among them and miracles in the land of Ham.

28     He sent darkness, and made the land dark; they did not rebel against his words.

29     He turned their waters into blood and caused their fish to die.

30     Their land swarmed with frogs, even in the chambers of their kings.

31     He spoke, and there came swarms of flies, and gnats throughout their country.

32     He gave them hail for rain, and fiery lightning bolts through their land.

33     He struck down their vines and fig trees, and shattered the trees of their country.

34     He spoke, and the locusts came, young locusts without number,

35     which devoured all the vegetation in their land and ate up the fruit of their ground.

36     He struck down all the firstborn in their land, the firstfruits of all their strength.

37     Then he brought out Israel with silver and gold, and there was none among his tribes who stumbled.

# UPROOTED

Thank You, Lord, for reminding me that I prosper wherever You send me. Just as the children of Israel prospered among the Egyptians, so I become fruitful even while I live in the midst of my enemies.

The Egyptians hated the Israelites and made their lives miserable. If You put me in a similar situation, I will call out to You just as they did. The Egyptians were a tool in Your hand to strengthen Your chosen ones. Even their devious ways prepared Your people to leave Egypt at the proper time. Use the actions of my adversaries to strengthen and prepare me to leave my comfort zone when You decide it's time for me to move.

You displayed Your power over the pantheon of Egyptian gods through the plagues. They worshipped Ra, the sun god, so You sent thick darkness upon the land. Every plague humbled one of the gods of Egypt. You demolished the myths of the Egyptians' idolatry and caused them to fear You more than they feared their idols.

When You remove me from the land of my enemies, display Your glory in a similar manner. Give them the ability to see You working on my behalf. Let them marvel at Your power. Send me out with silver and gold and with blessings even from my enemies.

In the transition of my move, cover me with Your protection. Holy Spirit, light my path and provide for me in abundance. Remember Your promises of loving kindness to me.

Because I trust You, I will come out with joy—even if the move uproots me from a place I love. I will sing of Your goodness and mercy while I grieve for love of the life I leave behind. I will gladly give up the best I have to obey You. If I must give up family or home or career, I will count the cost and confess that following You is worth leaving it all behind.

The land You promised Abraham You gave to the Israelites. There, they instituted Your statutes and observed Your laws. I want to live that way too. When You settle me in my new life, keep me from becoming distracted from worshipping You. Lead me in the path of righteousness, especially if You plant me in the presence of my enemies. Wherever You plant me, I will always praise You.

**38**  Egypt was glad when they departed, for dread of them had fallen upon it.

**39**  He spread a cloud for a covering, and fire to give light by night.

**40**  They asked, and he brought quail, and gave them bread from heaven in abundance.

**41**  He opened the rock, and water gushed out; it flowed through the desert like a river.

**42**  For he remembered his holy promise, and Abraham, his servant.

**43**  So he brought his people out with joy, his chosen ones with singing.

**44**  And he gave them the lands of the nations, and they took possession of the fruit of the peoples' toil,

**45**  that they might keep his statutes and observe his laws. Praise the Lord!

# MY PRAYER

_____

_____

_____

_____

_____

_____

_____

_____

_____

_____

_____

_____

_____

_____

_____

_____

_____

_____

_____

_____

_____

_____

_____

_____

_____

# Psalm 106:1–23

1   Praise the Lord! Oh give thanks to the Lord, for he is good, for his steadfast love endures forever!

2   Who can utter the mighty deeds of the Lord, or declare all his praise?

3   Blessed are they who observe justice, who do righteousness at all times!

4   Remember me, O Lord, when you show favor to your people; help me when you save them,

5   that I may look upon the prosperity of your chosen ones, that I may rejoice in the gladness of your nation, that I may glory with your inheritance.

6   Both we and our fathers have sinned; we have committed iniquity; we have done wickedness.

7   Our fathers, when they were in Egypt, did not consider your wondrous works; they did not remember the abundance of your steadfast love, but rebelled by the Sea, at the Red Sea.

8   Yet he saved them for his name's sake, that he might make known his mighty power.

9   He rebuked the Red Sea, and it became dry, and he led them through the deep as through a desert.

10   So he saved them from the hand of the foe and redeemed them from the power of the enemy.

11   And the waters covered their adversaries; not one of them was left.

12   Then they believed his words; they sang his praise.

13   But they soon forgot his works; they did not wait for his counsel.

14   But they had a wanton craving in the wilderness, and put God to the test in the desert;

# A MAN TO STAND

My heart and my lips overflow with praise to You, Lord. Your steadfast love endures forever! If the hearts and minds of everyone living were to praise You in one voice, that would provide only the faintest echo of the almighty "Hallelujah!" You deserve. How distressing that only a few of the billions alive think about You at all. You bless those who follow You because they see Your justice brings life. You give soul-deep peace to those who live in Your righteousness. Why then are they so blind to Your love for them?

Because You love Your people, You will save them, You will prosper Your chosen ones. I want to be among them when You make it happen. Give me the opportunity to look boldly at those who reject You as being distant and uncaring and say, "God's love is everlasting!"

We suffer because we and our forebearers have sinned. Appalling examples of our sinful ways fill the Bible. Forgive us, Lord, for down through the generations, we have worked hard to ignore the lessons these examples should teach us.

After You miraculously delivered the children of Israel from Egyptian slavery, the liberated slaves gave into the temptation to fear the Egyptian army. Where was their faith in You? Were they oblivious to the plagues You used to free them from Egyptian bondage?

You saved them from the Egyptian army by leading them through the Red Sea over dry ground through a safe passage. When the Egyptians attempted to cross the sea behind them, You mired the chariot wheels in mud and drowned them.

The Israelites, however, quickly forgot all Your work on their behalf and grumbled about the lack of meat. They wanted to return to Egypt because they didn't like the food! You gave them what they wanted. Along with meat, they got a wasting disease and leanness of soul.

They also rebelled against the leaders You had chosen for them. You saw the jealousy and scorn some people had for Moses and Aaron. You judged the rebellious leaders, their families, and their followers with holy fire and cleansing chasms.

You repeatedly displayed Your power, holiness, and determination to lead the children of Israel into a solemn, binding relationship with You.

15     he gave them what they asked, but sent a wasting disease among them.

16     When men in the camp were jealous of Moses and Aaron, the holy one of the Lord,

17     the earth opened and swallowed up Dathan, and covered the company of Abiram.

18     Fire also broke out in their company; the flame burned up the wicked.

19     They made a calf in Horeb and worshiped a metal image.

20     They exchanged the glory of God for the image of an ox that eats grass.

21     They forgot God, their Savior, who had done great things in Egypt,

22     wondrous works in the land of Ham, and awesome deeds by the Red Sea.

23     Therefore he said he would destroy them—had not Moses, his chosen one, stood in the breach before him, to turn away his wrath from destroying them.

When You met with them at Mount Horeb, Your holiness terrified them. You offered them a special relationship based on Your promises to Abraham and Your everlasting love. The children of Israel quickly agreed with Your plan, committing themselves and their children to worship and obey You.

Even after solemnly coming into a covenant with You, however, they turned away. Like a wild donkey, they showed a stubborn, headstrong determination to go their own way. They made a golden calf and worshipped the image of a grass-eating ox instead of the God who created them and the ox.

How this defiant act of contempt tested the quality of Your love! It created a gap in the hedge of protection You had erected around the Israelites. You, however, had already provided a man to stand in that breach. Moses offered his life for theirs. He reminded You that freeing the Israelites from slavery had displayed Your glory before the nations. He pleaded with You to turn away Your wrath from destroying them.

We're so like our forebearers; we fear circumstances instead of trusting You. We quickly forget Your loving care in our crises. We grumble and complain, never satisfied with what You give us. We criticize our leaders and exhibit a headstrong determination to go our own way.

Thank You that, just as Moses stood in the gap for the Israelites, Jesus stood in the greater breach for us all as He died on the cross. He took on Himself Your wrath and saved us from destruction. In a glorious display of Your everlasting love, Jesus closed the gap forever.

# Psalm 106:24–48

24  Then they despised the pleasant land, having no faith in his promise.

25  They murmured in their tents, and did not obey the voice of the Lord.

26  Therefore he raised his hand and swore to them that he would make them fall in the wilderness,

27  and would make their offspring fall among the nations, scattering them among the lands.

28  Then they yoked themselves to the Baal of Peor, and ate sacrifices offered to the dead;

29  they provoked the Lord to anger with their deeds, and a plague broke out among them.

30  Then Phinehas stood up and intervened, and the plague was stayed.

31  And that was counted to him as righteousness from generation to generation forever.

32  They angered him at the waters of Meribah, and it went ill with Moses on their account,

33  for they made his spirit bitter, and he spoke rashly with his lips.

34  They did not destroy the peoples, as the Lord commanded them,

35  but they mixed with the nations and learned to do as they did.

36  They served their idols, which became a snare to them.

37  They sacrificed their sons and their daughters to the demons;

38  they poured out innocent blood, the blood of their sons and daughters, whom they sacrificed to the idols of Canaan, and the land was polluted with blood.

# WITHOUT EXCUSE

Father, when I read this psalm, Your Spirit convicts me. The words tell of the faithlessness of the children of Israel; what I see are our own faithless ways.

Two years after freeing the Israelites from slavery, You brought them—with great promises of success—to the border of the pleasant land. Nonetheless, they had no faith in Your promises and refused to obey Your commands. How are we any different? When You say, "Trust me. Move forward. Take this territory," do we faithfully obey? I doubt You see much evidence of obedience.

The Israelites sank even lower when they settled in the land forty years later. They descended into idol worship. Because they failed to destroy the evil nations in the land, they joined them in demon worship. They burned their babies in the fires before the idols. They dedicated their sons and daughters to cult prostitution.

We do the same. We abort babies in the name of the god "convenience." We thrust our children into horrible situations in which they lose their innocence. Whether it is women selling their daughters or men producing homosexual pornography, children suffer greatly. We pour out innocent blood and pollute our land as the Israelites did. We prostitute ourselves in our desire for success and security.

The Israelites had less access to Your Word than we do, but You sent prophets to remind them of their promises to worship and obey You. The prophets described the consequences of the Israelites' rebellion, but the people failed to listen; all their purposes were rebellious against You.

We, however, are without excuse. We have the full record of the cost of breaking covenant with You. I wish I could say that having the Bible so readily available makes a difference to our willingness to faithfully obey You, but I doubt You see little evidence of that either.

Nevertheless, I have hope. Yes, we fail to grow in faith. Too often we do everything but obey You, but I see hope in this psalm. You punished the Israelites to correct them, not to destroy them. As You show us in Your Word, even when Your children break their covenant with You, You keep Your side of the agreement. Because of the abundance of Your steadfast love, You will rescue us. We are without excuse when You punish us, but we are not without hope when we repent. Save us, Lord.

**39** Thus they became unclean by their acts, and played the whore in their deeds.

**40** Then the anger of the Lord was kindled against his people, and he abhorred his heritage;

**41** he gave them into the hand of the nations, so that those who hated them ruled over them.

**42** Their enemies oppressed them, and they were brought into subjection under their power.

**43** Many times he delivered them, but they were rebellious in their purposes and were brought low through their iniquity.

**44** Nevertheless, he looked upon their distress, when he heard their cry.

**45** For their sake he remembered his covenant, and relented according to the abundance of his steadfast love.

**46** He caused them to be pitied by all those who held them captive.

**47** Save us, O Lord our God, and gather us from among the nations, that we may give thanks to your holy name and glory in your praise.

**48** Blessed be the Lord, the God of Israel, from everlasting to everlasting! And let all the people say, "Amen!" Praise the Lord!

# MY PRAYER

_____

_____

_____

_____

_____

_____

_____

_____

_____

_____

_____

_____

_____

_____

_____

_____

_____

_____

_____

_____

_____

_____

_____

# Psalm 107:1–22

1    Oh give thanks to the Lord, for he is good, for his steadfast love endures forever!

2    Let the redeemed of the Lord say so, whom he has redeemed from trouble

3    and gathered in from the lands, from the east and from the west, from the north and from the south.

4    Some wandered in desert wastes, finding no way to a city to dwell in;

5    hungry and thirsty, their soul fainted within them.

6    Then they cried to the Lord in their trouble, and he delivered them from their distress.

7    He led them by a straight way till they reached a city to dwell in.

8    Let them thank the Lord for his steadfast love, for his wondrous works to the children of men!

9    For he satisfies the longing soul, and the hungry soul he fills with good things.

10    Some sat in darkness and in the shadow of death, prisoners in affliction and in irons,

11    for they had rebelled against the words of God, and spurned the counsel of the Most High.

12    So he bowed their hearts down with hard labor; they fell down, with none to help.

13    Then they cried to the Lord in their trouble, and he delivered them from their distress.

14    He brought them out of darkness and the shadow of death, and burst their bonds apart.

# LOVE BEYOND COMPREHENSION

Lord, through the years, You have not always been my heart's passion. I have been fickle, foolish, and easily distracted. You, however, never lost Your passion for me. When I moved away from You in any direction, Your steadfast love drew me back, You gathered me into Your arms.

Once, I drifted away from You. I allowed laziness to separate us. Sleeping late was easier than getting up on Sunday morning to go to church. It took less energy to watch TV than to spend my personal time reading the Bible or talking to You.

As I did anything other than worship You, I discovered my joy had become ashes, complaining swallowed contentment, and bickering battled peace. I had allowed myself to wander into a desert waste. It didn't even bother me that I had broken our fellowship. With my "Whatever!" attitude, I intended to stay in the desert, but because You love me, You wouldn't allow that. Memories of sweet communion popped into my mind, birthing a hunger to read my Bible. Songs of praise played in my head, making me thirsty to worship You in church. I cried out to You, and You delivered me out of my distress. You led me back to fellowship with You and with my church family. You filled my parched soul with Your presence and satisfied my hunger with Your steadfast love.

Rebellion scarred my life, too. Even as You warned me away from the danger, I turned away from You and walked through the gate of the forbidden, lured by my impatient greed. A door of iron bars clanged shut behind me; bronze doors locked inside me. I soon regretted my decision, but it was too late. Many years of hard labor wore me down. No one helped me carry the load.

Finally, I came to the end of my endurance. Like a kitten clinging to a tree branch with only her front claws, I was helpless to save myself. You, however, did not forget me. While I slaved away, living my life for a cruel master, You came into the prison to carry me out. Like that kitten, You found me clinging to life by my fingernails. You said, "Let go, beloved, for I am here to catch you." Trusting myself had never led me to freedom, so I trusted You and let go. You burst the chains around my heart. You replaced that imitation life with life lived large, filled with eternal satisfaction. *You* did that for me.

**15**    Let them thank the Lord for his steadfast love, for his wondrous works to the children of men!

**16**    For he shatters the doors of bronze and cuts in two the bars of iron.

**17**    Some were fools through their sinful ways, and because of their iniquities suffered affliction;

**18**    they loathed any kind of food, and they drew near to the gates of death.

**19**    Then they cried to the Lord in their trouble, and he delivered them from their distress.

**20**    He sent out his word and healed them, and delivered them from their destruction.

**21**    Let them thank the Lord for his steadfast love, for his wondrous works to the children of men!

**22**    And let them offer sacrifices of thanksgiving, and tell of his deeds in songs of joy!

Lord, I want to rest in Your shadow instead of wandering in the desert or serving a slave master. I guard myself against those paths now, yet I often find other ways to leave Your side. Most insidious of all the paths away from You are the "little" sins that I excuse in myself: the white lie, the bit of gossip, the critical attitude. Their presence in my life makes Bible passages bitter food—undesired and unappetizing. They cut me off from the flow of Your Spirit's life. Nevertheless, You love me too much to leave me with this cancer eating at my soul.

You open my blind eyes to show me that even little sins are breaches of faith. Every time I turn temptation into sin, I shave away a bit of my life that pleases You. I grieve Your heart. I deaden my own heart, and Your voice becomes harder to hear. However, Your steadfast love is so enduring that Your Spirit stubbornly stays in my heart, providing a way out with every temptation, encouraging me to resist all the little sins.

In all my foolish ways, You draw me back to You with Your love. When I walk through the fire of sinful desires, the flames fail to consume me—because of Your love. As I pass through rivers of temptations, You save me from drowning. Who am I to be loved by You? The answer to that question eludes me, yet I know Your steadfast love works miracles in my life. Thank You.

# Psalm 107:23–43

23    Some went down to the sea in ships, doing business on the great waters;

24    they saw the deeds of the Lord, his wondrous works in the deep.

25    For he commanded and raised the stormy wind, which lifted up the waves of the sea.

26    They mounted up to heaven; they went down to the depths; their courage melted away in their evil plight;

27    they reeled and staggered like drunken men and were at their wits' end.

28    Then they cried to the Lord in their trouble, and he delivered them from their distress.

29    He made the storm be still, and the waves of the sea were hushed.

30    Then they were glad that the waters were quiet, and he brought them to their desired haven.

31    Let them thank the Lord for his steadfast love, for his wondrous works to the children of men!

32    Let them extol him in the congregation of the people, and praise him in the assembly of the elders.

33    He turns rivers into a desert, springs of water into thirsty ground,

34    a fruitful land into a salty waste, because of the evil of its inhabitants.

35    He turns a desert into pools of water, a parched land into springs of water.

36    And there he lets the hungry dwell, and they establish a city to live in;

37    they sow fields and plant vineyards and get a fruitful yield.

38    By his blessing they multiply greatly, and he does not let their livestock diminish.

# THOSE WHO GO DOWN TO THE SEA

Those who go down to the sea know the power of Your sovereign rule. In just a few minutes, a vicious storm can form and mighty winds can churn the water into massive waves capable of flipping a ship. Hearts quake and courage fails before Your wondrous works in the deep.

You are sovereign, Jehovah. You decide which ships will travel safely, and You deliver them to port. Ships struggle through horrible storms, sometimes limping into safe harbors. The more terrible the storm, the more grateful the sailors are to You for delivering them from the deep.

You display Your sovereignty on land just as You do at sea. When the people of a nation fill the cup of evil to the brim, You dry up life-giving rivers and stop the springs from flowing. Many times—unlike the sailors who see You in the sudden storm—people fail to see You in the slow, river-drying drought. While sailors quail before the storm's fury, farmers endure each day of cloudless sky without confessing that the iron sky is as much evidence of Your sovereign power as is a hurricane.

You test sailors on the sea and You judge the evil hearts of nations, yet You also see those who hunger and thirst for You. For those who seek You, You display Your sovereignty by turning deserts into well-watered lands. You send flowing springs bubbling up from parched ground. You establish them in a city and bless them with fruitful lives. You protect them when powerful rulers oppress them.

Lord, fill us with Your wisdom. Teach us that You are the King of kings. You desire to bless us as we acknowledge Your right to reign in our lives. You test our commitment to You with the storms of life. When we trust in You, You lead us into safe harbors. Those who refuse to bow to Your authority, however, find only judgment at Your throne. Let us be like those who go down to the sea and turn to You before the day of judgment.

**39** When they are diminished and brought low through oppression, evil, and sorrow,

**40** he pours contempt on princes and makes them wander in trackless wastes;

**41** but he raises up the needy out of affliction and makes their families like flocks.

**42** The upright see it and are glad, and all wickedness shuts its mouth.

**43** Whoever is wise, let him attend to these things; let them consider the steadfast love of the Lord.

# My Prayer

_____

_____

_____

_____

_____

_____

_____

_____

_____

_____

_____

_____

_____

_____

_____

_____

_____

_____

_____

_____

_____

_____

_____

_____

_____

# Psalm 108

1    My heart is steadfast, O God! I will sing and make melody with all my being!

2    Awake, O harp and lyre! I will awake the dawn!

3    I will give thanks to you, O Lord, among the peoples; I will sing praises to you among the nations.

4    For your steadfast love is great above the heavens; your faithfulness reaches to the clouds.

5    Be exalted, O God, above the heavens! Let your glory be over all the earth!

6    That your beloved ones may be delivered, give salvation by your right hand and answer me!

7    God has promised in his holiness: "With exultation I will divide up Shechem and portion out the Valley of Succoth.

8    Gilead is mine; Manasseh is mine; Ephraim is my helmet, Judah my scepter.

9    Moab is my washbasin; upon Edom I cast my shoe; over Philistia I shout in triumph."

10   Who will bring me to the fortified city? Who will lead me to Edom?

11   Have you not rejected us, O God? You do not go out, O God, with our armies.

12   Oh grant us help against the foe, for vain is the salvation of man!

13   With God we shall do valiantly; it is he who will tread down our foes.

# BEFORE THE BATTLE

Give thanks now? Give thanks when my enemies oppose me and the battle is yet to be fought? The victory is far from certain—yet I should praise You? My foes are confident they will win the battle. I see my future hanging in the balance. Up or down? The issue has yet to be decided.

Oh, yes! Now is the time to praise You. You prepared a steadfast heart in me to trust in You. I will greet the dawn with passionate praise. I will burst forth from my home and wake the neighbors with my thanksgiving. I will publish my praise abroad to all who will listen.

Praising You puts the battle in the right perspective. Yes, I want to win; I have done everything in my power to succeed. If, however, my foes defeat me, my wealth will disappear and my pride will lie in tatters, but Your amazing love and faithfulness will uphold me.

My enemies cannot destroy Your love for me. They cannot steal Your gift of salvation. The promises You gave me are based on Your holiness, so who could force You to break even the most insignificant one?

Yes, I have done my best to prepare, but You are the commander. None of my preparations will matter if You do not lead. I trust in You alone, not in myself or in any other person. I will fight, but You will tread down my foes. And Lord, win or lose, I will never cease to praise You.

People turn to You in their times of need, for You protect the poor, the weak, and all who have no one else to help them. Their own rulers may be callous to their problems, but You value all people who call out to You. Father, lead people to turn to You because their spiritual needs are greater than their physical needs will ever be. Please call them into Your kingdom before the last battle.

Righteous people in every nation will enjoy the blessings of Your kingdom. They will praise You, Father, with songs of thanksgiving and will thank You for sending Your Son to reign.

Oh how glorious that will be! Yet my heart rejoices most about one part of Your kingdom to come on earth: abundant food. Instead of the images of starving children I see today, I will see healthy bodies, active minds, and happy laughter abounding in children around the world. My mother's heart longs for that day to arrive.

# My Prayer

_____

_____

_____

_____

_____

_____

_____

_____

_____

_____

_____

_____

_____

_____

_____

_____

_____

_____

_____

_____

Your kingdom, Lord Jesus, is not a return to the garden of Eden. Not all humanity will give up its rebellion against You. Nevertheless, those who embrace You as their Lord and Savior will be blessed in You. Many people in every nation will call on Your Name.

Jehovah, God of Israel, only You could accomplish this wondrous thing. When Your kingdom comes, the whole earth will be filled with Your glory. You alone can force humanity into becoming a society in which social justice thrives. Your invincible power will restrain strong oppressors and the depraved. Until then, even as I fight this battle, I know You have won the war. At the victory celebration, I will rejoice with all who love You. We will sing, "Blessed be Your glorious name forever."

# Psalm 109:1–20

1    Be not silent, O God of my praise!

2    For wicked and deceitful mouths are opened against me, speaking against me with lying tongues.

3    They encircle me with words of hate, and attack me without cause.

4    In return for my love they accuse me, but I give myself to prayer.

5    So they reward me evil for good, and hatred for my love.

6    Appoint a wicked man against him; let an accuser stand at his right hand.

7    When he is tried, let him come forth guilty; let his prayer be counted as sin!

8    May his days be few; may another take his office!

9    May his children be fatherless and his wife a widow!

10   May his children wander about and beg, seeking food far from the ruins they inhabit!

11   May the creditor seize all that he has; may strangers plunder the fruits of his toil!

12   Let there be none to extend kindness to him, nor any to pity his fatherless children!

13   May his posterity be cut off; may his name be blotted out in the second generation!

14   May the iniquity of his fathers be remembered before the Lord, and let not the sin of his mother be blotted out!

15   Let them be before the Lord continually, that he may cut off the memory of them from the earth!

# BAD MEN

Lord, my five-year-old granddaughter came to me and told me with great conviction, "Nana, there really are bad men"; her innocence does not protect her from evil people in this world. Little girls, however, are not the only vulnerable ones. Because of sin, this world is a dangerous place for us all.

Just as some people embrace the good news that we can repent and be reconciled to You through Jesus, other people embrace Satan and his lies about personal power and freedom from all restraints. These others become enemies of Your children and hate everything for which they stand. They attack us only because we live our lives in praise of You. They accuse us of snobbery when we refuse to join them in riotous living. They are black holes absorbing all the love and good deeds we pour into their lives. They return hatred for love and evil for good.

Evil people have diabolical plans for Your children. They target us with campaigns of lies; they twist the truth and reinterpret the words we use so our community rejects us. They conspire to bring us to authorities with trumped-up charges and convince them that we are guilty. They plot to take away our wealth and our businesses and to kill us. They want to turn our wives into widows and make our children fatherless. Their passion is to remove even the memory of us from the world.

If these evil people would repent, You would forgive even all these horrors. After all, our sins were just as horrible and You forgave us. They, however, embrace opportunities to curse those You love instead of turning to You in repentance. They pursue those who humble themselves before You. Those who repent of their sins, they want to destroy.

Humility and confession horrify those who embrace evil. They wrap themselves in cursing to fend off Your Holy Spirit, who convicts them of their sins. They reject every opportunity of repentance You give them.

At the end, the last opportunity will be past, and their day of judgment will arrive. On the day they face the truth, all the evil deeds against Your people will fall on their heads. They will find only terror, justice, and judgment when they stand before Your throne. You will cleanse evil from all Your creation so little girls will no longer fear bad men.

**16**    For he did not remember to show kindness, but pursued the poor and needy and the brokenhearted, to put them to death.

**17**    He loved to curse; let curses come upon him! He did not delight in blessing; may it be far from him!

**18**    He clothed himself with cursing as his coat; may it soak into his body like water, like oil into his bones!

**19**    May it be like a garment that he wraps around him, like a belt that he puts on every day!

**20**    May this be the reward of my accusers from the Lord, of those who speak evil against my life!

# My Prayer

_____

_____

_____

_____

_____

_____

_____

_____

_____

_____

_____

_____

_____

_____

_____

_____

_____

_____

_____

_____

_____

_____

_____

_____

_____

# Psalm 109:21–31

21 But you, O God my Lord, deal on my behalf for your name's sake; because your steadfast love is good, deliver me!

22 For I am poor and needy, and my heart is stricken within me.

23 I am gone like a shadow at evening; I am shaken off like a locust.

24 My knees are weak through fasting; my body has become gaunt, with no fat.

25 I am an object of scorn to my accusers; when they see me, they wag their heads.

26 Help me, O Lord my God! Save me according to your steadfast love!

27 Let them know that this is your hand; you, O Lord, have done it!

28 Let them curse, but you will bless! They arise and are put to shame, but your servant will be glad!

29 May my accusers be clothed with dishonor; may they be wrapped in their own shame as in a cloak!

30 With my mouth I will give great thanks to the Lord; I will praise him in the midst of the throng.

31 For he stands at the right hand of the needy, to save him from those who condemn his soul to death.

# MY WOUNDED HEART

What am I doing standing in a court of law, God? The only law I have broken intentionally is the speed limit, yet here I stand, facing earnest, angry accusers who say I harmed them.

I am very confused. The charges make no sense to me. The good I did sounds like evil on their lips. Those I wanted to help have wounded my heart with these senseless allegations, and the scorn they heap on me scatters my thoughts. My confusion kills my appetite. My unintentional hunger strike wastes me away and leaves me weak. How can I go on?

My courage has leaked away with my strength. I fear my own shadow. Every sound startles me because I don't know what will happen next. My broken heart longs for peace. I want to return to the time when I found fulfillment in my life. I do not know how to fight, Lord, yet I am caught up in this battle.

Help me, O Lord my God! Straighten out this mess in such a miraculous way that even my opponents will have to confess You came to my rescue. Show them You will turn their curses into blessings. Provide an audience to see the way my accusers shame and dishonor themselves. I will tell the crowd You brought forth the facts, You displayed the truth, and You rescued me.

Please stand at my right hand now, as I face the judge. Save me from those who would condemn me to death. Deliver me for Your Name's sake.

# PSALM 110

1    The Lord says to my Lord: "Sit at my right hand, until I make your enemies your footstool."

2    The Lord sends forth from Zion your mighty scepter. Rule in the midst of your enemies!

3    Your people will offer themselves freely on the day of your power, in holy garments; from the womb of the morning, the dew of your youth will be yours.

4    The Lord has sworn and will not change his mind, "You are a priest forever after the order of Melchizedek."

5    The Lord is at your right hand; he will shatter kings on the day of his wrath.

6    He will execute judgment among the nations, filling them with corpses; he will shatter chiefs over the wide earth.

7    He will drink from the brook by the way; therefore he will lift up his head.

# Exalted King

Father, the words You speak to Your Son overwhelm me. Jesus Christ, my Lord and Savior, sits at Your right hand on His glorious throne while You humble His enemies. You prepare the staff of His royal office and send it out.

On earth, You assemble an army of people. They become His servants because they love Him. They set themselves apart, living holy lives with diligence and discipline. On the day You proclaim as His coronation day, they will willingly join and serve with the heavenly host.

Father, You promise that on Jesus' coronation day, He will have great power to overcome His enemies. The same power that created the universe—before the morning was born—will be His to ensure victory. His personal strength will equal the strength He had at the dawn of the universe.

Today, as Jesus sits at Your right hand, He attends to His responsibilities as Great High Priest, interceding for those He came to earth to save. While You are humbling His enemies, He is caring for us! You guard His Name while He shepherds His people. What tenderhearted love. What enduring compassion.

On the day You appoint, Father, Jesus' royal scepter will be a rod of iron. He will shatter kings and execute judgment. The corpses of His enemies will cover the earth. Even with the outpouring of His imperial wrath, His strength will be undiminished. You will restore His energy. You will lift His head to reign over all the earth.

Holy, holy, holy are You,
Lord God Almighty.
Let all the earth
Resound with Your glory.

# Psalm 111

1     Praise the Lord! I will give thanks to the Lord with my whole heart, in the company of the upright, in the congregation.

2     Great are the works of the Lord, studied by all who delight in them.

3     Full of splendor and majesty is his work, and his righteousness endures forever.

4     He has caused his wondrous works to be remembered; the Lord is gracious and merciful.

5     He provides food for those who fear him; he remembers his covenant forever.

6     He has shown his people the power of his works, in giving them the inheritance of the nations.

7     The works of his hands are faithful and just; all his precepts are trustworthy;

8     they are established forever and ever, to be performed with faithfulness and uprightness.

9     He sent redemption to his people; he has commanded his covenant forever. Holy and awesome is his name!

10     The fear of the Lord is the beginning of wisdom; all those who practice it have a good understanding. His praise endures forever!

# EVEN YOUR NAME IS HOLY

My life is all about You, God. You alone are worthy of all my praises. I eagerly join my brothers and sisters in church for the single purpose of joyfully praising You. Together, we wholeheartedly rejoice in Your greatness.

Your Word displays who You are. From the splendor of creation to the almighty power of the Messiah's resurrection, we delight in studying Your ways and works. We meditate on Your attributes—love, grace, mercy, justice, faithfulness, and holiness.

Your Word tells us even Your Name is holy. Yahweh, Adonai, Jehovah, Lord God Almighty, Father in heaven. In all Your Names, we see You are God and we are not. Why then do we speak Your Name so lightly? You seek a heart of loving reverence, not an attitude of superstitious fear when we speak of You. Nevertheless, I think even superstitious fear would be an improvement over the callous profanity that fills our mouths. Your Name should be a blessing when we speak it, and yet we use it to curse others and ourselves.

Your goodness and grace teach us to honor and respect You with the reverential fear You desire of us. Your mercies that are renewed every morning draw us to You. We become Your people because You redeemed us. You poured out Your righteous wrath, which we deserve, on Jesus. For that, we love You. Connect our love for You with a sensitivity to respect Your Name when we speak.

As we learn more about You and spend time in Your presence, change us into people who honor Your Name. Increase our wisdom as we obey Your commandments so our lips will be cleansed of curses. Reveal Yourself to us so our tongues and lives produce praise that endures. You are worthy of all praise.

# Psalm 112

1   Praise the Lord! Blessed is the man who fears the Lord, who greatly delights in his commandments!

2   His offspring will be mighty in the land; the generation of the upright will be blessed.

3   Wealth and riches are in his house, and his righteousness endures forever.

4   Light dawns in the darkness for the upright; he is gracious, merciful, and righteous.

5   It is well with the man who deals generously and lends; who conducts his affairs with justice.

6   For the righteous will never be moved; he will be remembered forever.

7   He is not afraid of bad news; his heart is firm, trusting in the Lord.

8   His heart is steady; he will not be afraid, until he looks in triumph on his adversaries.

9   He has distributed freely; he has given to the poor; his righteousness endures forever; his horn is exalted in honor.

10  The wicked man sees it and is angry; he gnashes his teeth and melts away; the desire of the wicked will perish!

# Miraculous Change

He worked in my home, Lord, and I never had a clue. He was knowledgeable, professional, and pleasant, and he fooled me completely. He had a secret, sinful life that eventually seared through the façade of civility and exposed his real character. He was a hypocrite. If he feared You at all, Father, it was with a craven terror inspired by the possibility that You would expose his true character.

Another man worked in my home as well. This man was also a pleasant, diligent worker. Sometimes, side by side, the two did their jobs. On the outside, they were similar, but You knew who they were inside their skin. The second man lived righteously. He feared You with reverent love. He delighted in studying Your Word and obeying Your commands.

Both men were gracious, but the hypocrite's soul was greedy and unmerciful. The righteous man gave generously and lived justly. When bad news came—as it does for the hypocrites and the righteous alike—You exposed the sinful life of the hypocrite, and his façade melted away. The life he had built for himself collapsed in the earthquake of consequences.

When bad news came to the righteous man, You led him along a radiant path. The faith his life displayed became a foundation for the road traveled by his children—the Way of Life. Because of his obedience, You will bless generations of his offspring. You will give him wealth—riches now, and enduring righteousness forever.

It's the choice everyone faces, Lord: craven terror or reverent love. Will someone build a wall to hide sins or fall in repentance before the cross? You died on that cross so everyone might, through the blood of Jesus, shed hypocrisy and live righteous lives. Oh Father, do not delay in miraculously changing the hypocrites into righteous people.

# Psalm 113

1     Praise the Lord! Praise, O servants of the Lord, praise the name of the Lord!

2     Blessed be the name of the Lord from this time forth and forevermore!

3     From the rising of the sun to its setting, the name of the Lord is to be praised!

4     The Lord is high above all nations, and his glory above the heavens!

5     Who is like the Lord our God, who is seated on high,

6     who looks far down on the heavens and the earth?

7     He raises the poor from the dust and lifts the needy from the ash heap,

8     to make them sit with princes, with the princes of his people.

9     He gives the barren woman a home, making her the joyous mother of children. Praise the Lord!

# WHY DO YOU CARE?

Hallelujah!

Who will praise You, Lord? Those who serve You with joy. Those who love You with their obedience. They will praise You from the moment they awaken until they close their eyes to sleep. In their dreams, they will call upon You.

Hallelujah!

Why do we servants praise You? Because You created this gloriously astonishing universe. The majesty of the solar system and the splendor of the galaxies reflect Your glory.

Infinity encompasses space. Eternity is the boundary of time. Our minds only vaguely grasp these truths, yet You sit beyond all dimensions described by time and space and reign over Your creation. Only You are worthy of our praise.

Once, we believed that the sun and stars revolved around the earth. You drew back the curtain of ignorance and allowed us to see the way our planet revolves around the sun. We discovered that the sun hurtles through space with the rest of our Milky Way galaxy. You showed us that the universe expands continuously; our galaxy moves away from all the others. We cannot comprehend the elegant harmonies of the night sky.

So what is man that You are mindful of him and the son of man that You care for him? We live on a backwater planet of a third-rate sun. We survive in the dust of an ash heap. We tiny specks of humanity are altogether poor and needy. We have nothing that would call us to Your attention, nothing to recommend us for Your favor. Nevertheless, You look down, You reach out, You step in, and You delight to raise us above our place. You lift us out of the mire and into Your kingdom. Not one of our needs is too small, none of our crises too large for You to deliver us.

We praise You because You love us even though we fail You. You renew Your mercies for us every morning. Your grace, through our Lord Jesus Christ, sustains us. Your Holy Spirit's power transforms us into the likeness of Your Son. These miracles far outshine the creation of the galaxies. For these astonishing miracles, we most profoundly praise You.

# PSALM 114

1 When Israel went out from Egypt, the house of Jacob from a people of strange language,

2 Judah became his sanctuary, Israel his dominion.

3 The sea looked and fled; Jordan turned back.

4 The mountains skipped like rams, the hills like lambs.

5 What ails you, O sea, that you flee? O Jordan, that you turn back?

6 O mountains, that you skip like rams? O hills, like lambs?

7 Tremble, O earth, at the presence of the Lord, at the presence of the God of Jacob,

8 who turns the rock into a pool of water, the flint into a spring of water.

# WORKING WONDERS

Your ways astonish me, Lord. Among the many routes You could have chosen to take the Israelites as they left Egypt's slavery, You took the one that led over the dry floor of the Red Sea. Forty years later, that road led them dry shod across the bed of the flooding Jordan River and into the Promised Land.

The waters of the Red Sea piled up, not like a great glacier but like a crystalline wall of rock towering over the children of Israel as they took that final step into freedom. What did the waters see? They saw You working a miracle more marvelous than that of the waves standing on end. They saw You delivering Jacob's family. That promise You kept held the seed of creation's deliverance.

The Jordan River retreated for thirty miles from the feet of the ark-carrying priests. Why did it flee? It was Your power—the same power that caused death to flee on Easter morning when You raised Your Son to glory—that removed the water. Nothing can restrain Your redemption plan.

Just as the hills skipped like lambs when You showed Yourself at Sinai, the mountains will abandon their place when Your Son returns to reign. The sea will disappear, and rivers will dry up. A new river will flow from the threshold of Your temple—pure, life-giving water for a thirsty world.

Mountains and rivers, oceans and hills, all the earth watches You work the wonders of deliverance. With eager expectation, it waits for the day when You will deliver it from the bondage of decay. God of all wonders, hasten the day when You deliver creation from its awful curse.

# PSALM 115

1   Not to us, O Lord, not to us, but to your name give glory, for the sake of your steadfast love and your faithfulness!

2   Why should the nations say, "Where is their God?"

3   Our God is in the heavens; he does all that he pleases.

4   Their idols are silver and gold, the work of human hands.

5   They have mouths, but do not speak; eyes, but do not see.

6   They have ears, but do not hear; noses, but do not smell.

7   They have hands, but do not feel; feet, but do not walk; and they do not make a sound in their throat.

8   Those who make them become like them; so do all who trust in them.

9   O Israel, trust in the Lord! He is their help and their shield.

10  O house of Aaron, trust in the Lord! He is their help and their shield.

11  You who fear the Lord, trust in the Lord! He is their help and their shield.

12  The Lord has remembered us; he will bless us; he will bless the house of Israel; he will bless the house of Aaron;

13  he will bless those who fear the Lord, both the small and the great.

14  May the Lord give you increase, you and your children!

15  May you be blessed by the Lord, who made heaven and earth!

16  The heavens are the Lord's heavens, but the earth he has given to the children of man.

17  The dead do not praise the Lord, nor do any who go down into silence.

18  But we will bless the Lord from this time forth and forevermore. Praise the Lord!

# DESIGNED TO WORSHIP

Glory to Your Name! Glory to Your Name, Almighty God! You are God, steadfast in love and faithfulness.

When You created humanity, You designed the ability and the desire to worship into the fiber of our being. When we rebelled, we warped that desire and built false gods. Every society, every culture creates gods to worship; most of them construct idols to represent their gods. We go to extremes in our rebellion against You.

When we opened the door to sin, the ability to worship became a double curse to humanity. In life, the false god worshippers become like their idols. The idols have unspeaking mouths, unhearing ears, and no sense of smell or taste. They have unfeeling hands and unmoving feet; they cannot make even the faintest sound. Likewise, the ones who worship idols are unable to call out to You, hear Your voice, or taste and see You are good. They cannot reach out and share Your love with others, go to serve others in Your Name, or utter groans of repentance. No, they become as dead to You as the idols are dead to the loveliness of Your created world.

Even worse is the horror of the doubled curse. In death, those who chose to live in rebellion against You and who refused Your gift of forgiveness will spend eternity in hell. Deprived of all the senses we enjoy, they will not be able even to groan in agony. Like an earthworm writhing on red-hot coals, they will be unable to escape hell's torment. No light, no joy, no laughter—only endless, inexpressible pain.

Oh, but we have a choice! Because of Your steadfast love and faithfulness, we can choose to worship You. Thank You, Father, that Jesus' sacrifice removed hell from our future. Because He took our punishment, we can freely, gladly, joyously do what You designed us to do—worship You.

At all times and in every way, we praise You. Everywhere we turn our eyes, we see Your miracles. Our ears are tuned to hear the faintest whisper of Your voice. Our hands and feet are busily engaged in working as You direct. Even the smallest sounds in our throats are anthems of praise to You.

And oh, the glory of it—we become like You! The more we worship You, the more like You we become. How could we not become like You? You bless us with Your presence—the true God—sharing in our lives and stripping away our sinful habits.

# My Prayer

_____

_____

_____

_____

_____

_____

_____

_____

_____

_____

_____

_____

_____

_____

_____

_____

_____

_____

_____

_____

_____

You steadily increase our likeness to Your Son, refining our sin-smeared, out-of-focus image into the clear likeness of Jesus. The more like Him we become, the more of a blessing we become to our families and others around us.

Yes, Lord, You designed us to worship. And though the dead cannot, the rebellious will not, and the careless do not, we worship You. To You be the honor and the glory. We praise You, Lord.

# PSALM 116

1    I love the Lord, because he has heard my voice and my pleas for mercy.

2    Because he inclined his ear to me, therefore I will call on him as long as I live.

3    The snares of death encompassed me; the pangs of Sheol laid hold on me; I suffered distress and anguish.

4    Then I called on the name of the Lord: "O Lord, I pray, deliver my soul!"

5    Gracious is the Lord, and righteous; our God is merciful.

6    The Lord preserves the simple; when I was brought low, he saved me.

7    Return, O my soul, to your rest; for the Lord has dealt bountifully with you.

8    For you have delivered my soul from death, my eyes from tears, my feet from stumbling;

9    I will walk before the Lord in the land of the living.

10    I believed, even when I spoke, "I am greatly afflicted";

11    I said in my alarm, "All mankind are liars."

12    What shall I render to the Lord for all his benefits to me?

13    I will lift up the cup of salvation and call on the name of the Lord,

14    I will pay my vows to the Lord in the presence of all his people.

15    Precious in the sight of the Lord is the death of his saints.

16    O Lord, I am your servant; I am your servant, the son of your maidservant. You have loosed my bonds.

# THE GREAT AND TERRIBLE DAY OF THE LORD

How merciful You are, Lord. My great and terrible day of the Lord has passed. Before that day, I was careless in my arrogance; I felt free to choose a life outside Your law. Like Scrooge in *The Christmas Carol*, I was insensible to sins' chains of slavery, indifferent to my own warped and twisted depravity. Yet on that great and terrible day, no ghost appeared; You sent Your Holy Spirit, who opened my eyes. I saw myself clothed in rags of rebellious pride, shackled to sins of greed and lust, scrounging in garbage pits for love, and planting poison seeds of wickedness all around me.

*So what?* I thought. *I have a free will. I can live like this if I want to.*

Then Your Spirit lifted the fog. At my feet, I saw the crumbling edge of a cliff. Slowly, I crept toward the edge. The snares of death reached out to pull me over. Panic seized me as I tried and failed to scramble back from the approaching plunge.

*It's true,* I thought. *My choices have consequences. Hell is real.*

Your Spirit showed me the way out. Redemption stood before me—Your Son, Jesus Christ—dressed in dazzling purity, unapproachable by a sinner like me. His face was stern, but his eyes drew me with overwhelming love, and His hands were outstretched in welcome.

How great became that terrible day! I cried to You for mercy. I prayed for You to deliver my soul. You heard my cry. You answered my prayer. You saved me.

The day I discovered I was a slave to the fear of death brought me anguish and distress as You showed me my sin and my destination. Praise You, Lord! I responded to Your call, repented of my sins, and turned to You. Then my soul found rest, my life gained purpose, and my heart crowned You king. You gave Your all for me, Jesus, that I might have all in You.

Therefore, I love You! How could I not? I will call on You with praise and thanksgiving for all my days. Instead of stumbling, my feet dance. Instead of shedding tears, my eyes radiate joy. I will call on You until the day arrives when my body no longer anchors my spirit to the earth.

**17**  I will offer to you the sacrifice of thanksgiving and call on the name of the Lord.

**18**  I will pay my vows to the Lord in the presence of all his people,

**19**  in the courts of the house of the Lord, in your midst, O Jerusalem. Praise the Lord!

The future great and terrible day of the Lord will be no terrible day for me because death and hell will not await me. You will walk with me where they can never approach. I will walk with You, my Lord, in the land of the living. There I will continue to serve You, delighting to offer praise and thanksgiving with all who call on the Name of Jesus. No longer bound by my old sinful nature, I will offer my pure obedience and display more magnificently the love I found on the great and wonderful day of the Lord.

# Psalm 117

1     Praise the Lord, all nations! Extol him, all peoples!

2     For great is his steadfast love toward us, and the faithfulness of the Lord endures forever.

*Praise the Lord!*

# Extravagant Praise

Lord, several thousand years ago, You put the desire in the heart of the psalmist to write a command to all the nations: "Praise the Lord!" The writer of the psalm required no solemn chant to be murmured in a hushed whisper. This God-fearing worshipper desired the nations around the world to praise You passionately, extravagantly, and with great enthusiasm. His zeal to see everyone praise You led him to address the people in communities of every size. He commanded both Jew and non-Jew to praise You with exuberance.

Everyone has reason to praise You. Your steadfast love overcomes the evil that saturates every nation and all people. Your faithfulness endures forever; You keep all Your promises. As the earth turns on its axis, in every nation where morning dawns and evening fades, You bring forth the song of salvation.

Where, then, are the nations to praise You? The loudest echoes of passionate praise come from sporting events. Wild cheering comes from arenas hosting the newest pop stars. Enthusiastic acclaim resounds from the supporters of the politician who won the latest election. Right now, no nation praises You.

Nevertheless, a day is coming when You will banish sin and death. On that day, the command for all nations to praise You will be joyfully, passionately fulfilled. Every tribe will extol Your Name. All nations will be overwhelmingly thankful for Your love and Your faithfulness. What a day of rejoicing that will be!

# Psalm 118:1–18

1   Oh give thanks to the Lord, for he is good; for his steadfast love endures forever!

2   Let Israel say, "His steadfast love endures forever."

3   Let the house of Aaron say, "His steadfast love endures forever."

4   Let those who fear the Lord say, "His steadfast love endures forever."

5   Out of my distress I called on the Lord; the Lord answered me and set me free.

6   The Lord is on my side; I will not fear. What can man do to me?

7   The Lord is on my side as my helper; I shall look in triumph on those who hate me.

8   It is better to take refuge in the Lord than to trust in man.

9   It is better to take refuge in the Lord than to trust in princes.

10   All nations surrounded me; in the name of the Lord I cut them off!

11   They surrounded me, surrounded me on every side; in the name of the Lord I cut them off!

12   They surrounded me like bees; they went out like a fire among thorns; in the name of the Lord I cut them off!

13   I was pushed hard, so that I was falling, but the Lord helped me.

14   The Lord is my strength and my song; he has become my salvation.

15   Glad songs of salvation are in the tents of the righteous: "The right hand of the Lord does valiantly,

16   the right hand of the Lord exalts, the right hand of the Lord does valiantly!"

17   I shall not die, but I shall live, and recount the deeds of the Lord.

18   The Lord has disciplined me severely, but he has not given me over to death.

# STEADFAST LOVE

We thank You, Lord, for we know You are good. We trust in You for Your steadfast love endures forever.

Those You freed from the slavery of sin confess, "Your steadfast love endures forever."

Those who live to worship and praise You declare, "Your steadfast love endures forever."

Those who know Your great majesty proclaim, "Your steadfast love endures forever."

We have all had seasons when doubt attacked us, when loneliness surrounded us, when emptiness dropped away in front of our feet. Though friends fled and enemies gathered, we took up the battle. We gathered our faith, put on our courage, and shouted, "The Lord is on my side. I will not fear!"

Should we fear those who hate us simply because they can put our bodies to death? No, for they cannot separate us from You or Your love.

Should we be silenced by those who feel threatened when we praise You? No, even when surrounded by their contempt, we will stand in Your Name and cut them off.

Should we withdraw from displaying Your grace and love when some violently reject our message? No, because You are the only source of salvation. We will hold You up until the day when all humanity will confess, "Jesus is Lord."

We will always rejoice that Your steadfast love endures forever.

# PSALM 118:19–29

19     Open to me the gates of righteousness, that I may enter through them and give thanks to the Lord.

20     This is the gate of the Lord; the righteous shall enter through it.

21     I thank you that you have answered me and have become my salvation.

22     The stone that the builders rejected has become the cornerstone.

23     This is the Lord's doing; it is marvelous in our eyes.

24     This is the day that the Lord has made; let us rejoice and be glad in it.

25     Save us, we pray, O Lord ! O Lord , we pray, give us success!

26     Blessed is he who comes in the name of the Lord! We bless you from the house of the Lord.

27     The Lord is God, and he has made his light to shine upon us. Bind the festal sacrifice with cords, up to the horns of the altar!

28     You are my God, and I will give thanks to you; you are my God; I will extol you.

29     Oh give thanks to the Lord, for he is good; for his steadfast love endures forever!

# THE OPEN GATES

Lord Jesus, You opened the gates of righteousness for us by Your sacrifice on the cross. Seldom do I dwell on and appreciate the implications of those open gates. So often, I bring my needs quickly—sometimes frantically—before the throne of God. I rush through the gates without reflecting on the enormous price You paid to throw them open.

Holy Spirit, keep me from prayers so routine that I take access to God's throne for granted. Never let me become so thoughtless that I treat the privilege of bringing my needs before our Father as if I were approaching some kind of heavenly vending machine—put in a prayer, take out a blessing. Keep me aware that Jesus Christ is the only way to the Father's presence. I want to marvel always over this amazing gift: the gates of righteousness are open! I desire to rejoice in the presence of our Father as I exclaim over the day that Jesus threw open the gates.

Lord Jesus, You are God; Your death and resurrection brought the Light of Life and illuminated the path to reconciliation with our Father. I have nothing You have not given me, but I lay all that I am on Your altar. I wrap this gift in praise and thanksgiving, grateful that the gates of righteousness into the presence of God will always be open to me.

# Psalm 119:1–8 (Alef)

1   Blessed are those whose way is blameless, who walk in the law of the Lord!

2   Blessed are those who keep his testimonies, who seek him with their whole heart,

3   who also do no wrong, but walk in his ways!

4   You have commanded your precepts to be kept diligently.

5   Oh that my ways may be steadfast in keeping your statutes!

6   Then I shall not be put to shame, having my eyes fixed on all your commandments.

7   I will praise you with an upright heart, when I learn your righteous rules.

8   I will keep your statutes; do not utterly forsake me!

# How Do I Know?

"How do I know what God wants me to do?" a new Christian asks.

My heart leaps for joy when I hear that question, Lord. Now I can share with her the love I have for Your Word.

I pick up my Bible and put it in her hands. I tell this baby-in-Christ the words You have given me: "To know what God wants, you have to know God. This book will teach you about Him. The part called the New Testament contains wonderful accounts of Jesus' life and work on earth. It gives you the history of the early church and establishes God's plan and purpose for you now that you are part of His family."

Father, if we had only the New Testament, we would be abundantly blessed but would not have known as much about You. Thank You for leaving us the Old Testament too. I want this new Christian to know everything the Bible tells us about You, so I tell her, "Study the Old Testament too. You will get a beautiful picture of the immense scope of God's love, mercy, grace, and justice. In its pages, you will find some rules that do not apply to us who live under the new covenant, but you will see God in all its pages. In it, He speaks to His chosen people, divinely judges what is right, and lays down laws that lead to blameless living.

"Seek out God in the Bible. Study the ways through the centuries that God has revealed His will. That will teach you to recognize His voice and to understand what He wants you to do."

Lord, open her eyes and give her understanding. Yes, and, may *I* never lose my hunger for Your Word. Make it always as new and as fresh to me as it is to the person who reads it for the first time. When I read Your Word, my heart always overflows with reasons to praise You. Lord, please let me always experience the freshness of Your Word.

# Psalm 119:9–16 (Bet)

9   How can a young man keep his way pure? By guarding it according to your word.

10  With my whole heart I seek you; let me not wander from your commandments!

11  I have stored up your word in my heart, that I might not sin against you.

12  Blessed are you, O Lord; teach me your statutes!

13  With my lips I declare all the rules of your mouth.

14  In the way of your testimonies I delight as much as in all riches.

15  I will meditate on your precepts and fix my eyes on your ways.

16  I will delight in your statutes; I will not forget your word.

# No Forgetting

"Your word have I hid in my heart that I might not sin against you" (Psalm 119:11 KJV). Lord, I memorized that verse while still a child, when memorizing was easy. My mind stored that gem deep in my brain. Over the years, Your Spirit has reminded me of that verse, prompting me to memorize even more verses. Now I find memorizing anything—including Your Word—difficult. I forget much more easily than I remember.

Youth is the time for learning and seeking; it is the time when the need for guarding his heart should be uppermost in a young man's mind. Seldom, however, does one of them seek You with his whole heart; they are young and seek to understand life and to find their place in it.

Father, provide young men with mature, godly mentors who will walk beside them and guide them into Your Word. Godly people have learned Your statutes; prompt them to declare these words to young men. They know the trustworthiness of Your promises. Give them the words and opportunities to share with young men their own stories of Your love and faithfulness. Let Your glory so radiate through them that they learn to delight in Your Word. Then, Lord, when they grow old, they will treasure Your Word that they hid in their hearts and teach it to their children.

# Psalm 119:17–24 (Gimel)

17    Deal bountifully with your servant, that I may live and keep your word.

18    Open my eyes, that I may behold wondrous things out of your law.

19    I am a sojourner on the earth; hide not your commandments from me!

20    My soul is consumed with longing for your rules at all times.

21    You rebuke the insolent, accursed ones, who wander from your commandments.

22    Take away from me scorn and contempt, for I have kept your testimonies.

23    Even though princes sit plotting against me, your servant will meditate on your statutes.

24    Your testimonies are my delight; they are my counselors.

# THE WINDS BLOW

The winds blow harder, Lord.

I stand on the same foundation as always. Your commands order my days, and I study Your Word to know and understand those things You have declared to be right and true. I listen for Your voice so I might learn Your will. I meditate on the laws You have decreed. My heart delights in all You are and in the way of life I find in the Bible. My passion to grow in displaying Your glory increases as I study Your Word.

While I cooperate with You to become more like Jesus, the winds of the world blow harder in the opposite direction. Unspeakable things that once hid in dark corners and under brown paper covers now parade in the streets and boldly shove their way into our home. The insolent wander from Your way, and the arrogant ignore You altogether. I have become a stranger in my own country. Even our highest leaders—political and cultural—give approval to the most horrible sins with their words and lifestyles.

Lord, my strength to stand against this windstorm comes only from You. As it intensifies to drive me from my sure foundation, I depend entirely on You to hold me fast. Protect me from the scorn and contempt that buffet me. Fulfill my heart's longing to see my country humbly bowing before You. In Your generous grace, allow me to live to see the wind change directions. Let it become a gentle breeze that whispers of everlasting life in You instead of blowing the destructive force of death. Yes, Lord, let a new wind blow, the wind of the Holy Spirit, so we might all see a glorious day of salvation and praise You for Your grace.

# Psalm 119:25–32 (Dalet)

25  My soul clings to the dust; give me life according to your word!

26  When I told of my ways, you answered me; teach me your statutes!

27  Make me understand the way of your precepts, and I will meditate on your wondrous works.

28  My soul melts away for sorrow; strengthen me according to your word!

29  Put false ways far from me and graciously teach me your law!

30  I have chosen the way of faithfulness; I set your rules before me.

31  I cling to your testimonies, O Lord; let me not be put to shame!

32  I will run in the way of your commandments when you enlarge my heart!

# A Life Worth Living

Lord, no matter how physically painful or emotionally traumatic my life becomes, I cling to it. Even in the worst moments, I want to live. However, I want my life to have value, to please You, so my foundation is Your Word. I explain my troubles to You, rehearse my problems before You, and search the Bible to find Your answers. Your Word gives me more than answers. I find in it Your abundant love, Your sustaining power.

Father, even though I have only scratched the surface of Your wisdom, You show me ways to live in peace and give me help to overcome. I hunger for more wisdom and guidance from You. It grieves me that Your Spirit is not able to show me deeper truths in the Bible. Like the apostle Paul told the people in the church in Corinth, You can show me only the simple, easy precepts. I lack the spiritual maturity to understand anything else.

Lord Jesus, please give me the capacity beyond my natural abilities to understand the truth You have given us in the Bible. Keep me from following the words of false teachers or from choosing the worldly wisdom of any other gospel. I commit myself again to the way of faithfulness: following Your rules, hearing and obeying Your will, and passionately pursuing a life of holiness.

I can succeed only if You fill me with Your power, Holy Spirit, so expand my abilities to perceive and live out Your truth. That will make my life worth living.

# Psalm 119:33–40 (He)

---

33    Teach me, O Lord, the way of your statutes; and I will keep it to the end.

34    Give me understanding, that I may keep your law and observe it with my whole heart.

35    Lead me in the path of your commandments, for I delight in it.

36    Incline my heart to your testimonies, and not to selfish gain!

37    Turn my eyes from looking at worthless things; and give me life in your ways.

38    Confirm to your servant your promise, that you may be feared.

39    Turn away the reproach that I dread, for your rules are good.

40    Behold, I long for your precepts; in your righteousness give me life!

# My Heart Would Break

Lord, I sense I am soon to face a test to the breaking point, a test like Job's, one that displays Your glory to the angels and to everyone who hears the story. If that is true, I desperately need Your help.

Teach me the right way to follow Your rules so I can continue in Your path until the test is over.

Give me understanding so I can see beyond the pain and distress and keep my heart firmly planted in You.

Lead me as my path goes through flood and flame.

Bend my heart to delight in being broken and poured out for You, not selfish and greedy for gain.

Focus my eyes determinedly to Your path before me regardless of the circumstances, and keep my feet following where You lead.

Confirm to me Your promise. You said You would never leave me or forsake me. Show Your compassion to the lost by the way I live, serve You, and serve others.

Turn away the scorn of people whose eyes are blinded and who completely reject You.

Because Jesus' crucifixion reconciled me to You, I have eternal life. Thank You! You will never fail me, but I might fail this test. If You know I will fail it, remove me from the earth. My heart would break if I should fail it and so dishonor Your Name. Prepare me for the test, Lord.

# Psalm 119:41–48 (Vav)

41   Let your steadfast love come to me, O Lord, your salvation according to your promise;

42   then shall I have an answer for him who taunts me, for I trust in your word.

43   And take not the word of truth utterly out of my mouth, for my hope is in your rules.

44   I will keep your law continually, forever and ever,

45   and I shall walk in a wide place, for I have sought your precepts.

46   I will also speak of your testimonies before kings and shall not be put to shame,

47   for I find my delight in your commandments, which I love.

48   I will lift up my hands toward your commandments, which I love, and I will meditate on your statutes.

# ABSOLUTE TRUTH

Lord, sometimes the glory of Your Word astonishes me. On every page, I see Your love poured into humanity. I see the promises You make and know You always honor them. The holiness of the Bible causes me to pay close attention to what You tell me in its pages.

Some people would say I spend too much time studying Your Word. How easily I can reply! The Bible contains absolute truth—not the weak, cheap "truth" of everyone doing anything he or she desires. If You were to take the Bible away from me, I would be ignorant of the way my life measures up to what You, as divine judge, have ruled to be right. I would act so foolishly in trying to find the right on my own. Just the idea of not having the Bible appalls me. I desire always to know and obey Your commands. I would much rather please You than stumble along, attempting to meet everyone else's ideals of truth.

Father, I will look for opportunities to share Your Word with others. I will speak to people about Your abiding love and Your desire to see everyone experience eternal life through Jesus Christ. I cherish this wonderful news, and I delight in offering Your gift to those who have not yet accepted it.

Oh, Lord, keep me thankful for Your Word. I don't ever want to take it for granted. Keep the Bible in my hands and my heart. Lead me to glory always in its glory, the written Word of God.

# Psalm 119:49–56 (Zayin)

49  Remember your word to your servant, in which you have made me hope.

50  This is my comfort in my affliction, that your promise gives me life.

51  The insolent utterly deride me, but I do not turn away from your law.

52  When I think of your rules from of old, I take comfort, O Lord.

53  Hot indignation seizes me because of the wicked, who forsake your law.

54  Your statutes have been my songs in the house of my sojourning.

55  I remember your name in the night, O Lord, and keep your law.

56  This blessing has fallen to me, that I have kept your precepts.

# Climbing Out

Look at me, Lord. Here I am, frustrated, aggravated, humiliated—afflicted. I reacted to someone telling me I had made a mistake. Yes, I spoke sharply, my sinful nature rising once again out of the grave. Why do I fall into that sin so often? Why must I always defend myself over the most trivial matters? Why must I always be right? I am most indignant over my unwillingness to accept responsibility for the mistake. In so small a matter, who cares who made the mistake? Can I not love this person enough to accept the responsibility regardless of who was wrong? Why do I foolishly defend myself, putting my pride on display?

Your Spirit convicts me of this sin, but my conscience condemns me, telling me I will never overcome this sin pattern. I refuse, however, to listen to the condemnation. Instead, I will remember that You are my God, and I will take hope in Your Word. I am a new creature because You gave me a new life. Climbing out of this sin rut will not be easy. Nevertheless, just as You have in the past, You will give me the desire and the ability to overcome. I refuse to turn away from Your Word in despair; instead, I throw myself into Your arms.

No one else can help me. Holy Spirit, strengthen my spirit day and night. Remind me of the help You have given me in the past. You blessed me then, and You will bless me now. Thank You.

# Psalm 119:57–64 (Heth)

57  The Lord is my portion; I promise to keep your words.

58  I entreat your favor with all my heart; be gracious to me according to your promise.

59  When I think on my ways, I turn my feet to your testimonies;

60  I hasten and do not delay to keep your commandments.

61  Though the cords of the wicked ensnare me, I do not forget your law.

62  At midnight I rise to praise you, because of your righteous rules.

63  I am a companion of all who fear you, of those who keep your precepts.

64  The earth, O Lord , is full of your steadfast love; teach me your statutes!

# COPPER PENNIES

Years ago, I decided to listen when You called me to come to You, and I came in the simple faith of a child. I was not mature enough to understand the magnitude of that call, but I knew one undeniable, unshakable fact: that day, I became Your child, and You became my God and Father.

Years passed. I read Your Bible, listened to it taught at church, and saw my parents live according to it at home. Your Word guided my steps, for I found Your righteous ways in its pages. Then You opened my eyes to another level of knowing You. I discovered that giving my heart to You was only the beginning, not the end. As my Father and my King, You claimed not only my heart but also my complete obedience.

I tried to walk in this new light, but I found I had a serious problem: complete obedience was beyond my ability to give. Frustrated, I asked, "You gave me the desire to obey You and to live a holy life. How can I do it?"

I asked for knowledge, Lord—copper pennies—and You gave me golden coins! You turned my eyes to look within, and there I found Your Spirit. He had been present since the day I gave You my heart. He lives in me and makes Your power available to me to fulfill Your commands. I had been depending on my own mortal weakness when I could have leaned on Your almighty strength.

Now, I delight to do Your will. I trust Your Spirit to guide me and give me the power and the strength to obey. What I could not do by myself, the Holy Spirit and I can do together. Now, I search Your Word without fear of failing You. After all, it's not only the earth that is full of Your love; Your loving Spirit fills my heart with it as well. He fuels my life with love to display Your glory.

# Psalm 119:65–72 (Teth)

65   You have dealt well with your servant, O Lord, according to your word.

66   Teach me good judgment and knowledge, for I believe in your commandments.

67   Before I was afflicted I went astray, but now I keep your word.

68   You are good and do good; teach me your statutes.

69   The insolent smear me with lies, but with my whole heart I keep your precepts;

70   their heart is unfeeling like fat, but I delight in your law.

71   It is good for me that I was afflicted, that I might learn your statutes.

72   The law of your mouth is better to me than thousands of gold and silver pieces.

# GOLDEN COINS

Father, You promised that if I listened to Wisdom's call from Your Word and obeyed her discipline, You would cause me to live securely and not fear danger. You have kept that promise repeatedly. The protection You give me in every threatening circumstance reminds me to depend on You and not on myself. You are God and I am not.

You refresh my spirit as I read of Your love and tender care, but the more I learn of You in the Bible, the more I sense the great gap between knowing what Your Word *says* and understanding what it *means*. My ignorance appalls me. I want to understand Your glorious plans for creation that rest on Jesus Christ. Grant that my love for Jesus will abound more and more with wisdom and discernment as I study Your Word so I can understand and agree with the excellencies You've written in its pages.

Forgive me for the times when what I understood of Your Word only puffed me up with pride. That "knowledge" did nothing to help me, and it made others feel inferior. Holy Spirit, ingrain in my soul a gratitude for Your gracious favor. Only because of Your goodness and great love for me do I understand the smallest mystery.

I know it's impossible for me to learn anything when pride in what I *think* I know already makes my heart callous and unfeeling, so please protect me from arrogance. I want always to be teachable. The more You show me, the hungrier I am to learn more—more of You and more of Your plan. My desire is to see Your will done on earth as it is in heaven. No treasury of gold and silver coins can buy satisfaction of my heart's longing. Your Spirit's teaching delights me as no earthly treasure can. Renew my mind as I study Your Word so I can align myself with Your good, pure, and perfect plan.

# Psalm 119:73–80 (Yodh)

73   Your hands have made and fashioned me; give me understanding that I may learn your commandments.

74   Those who fear you shall see me and rejoice, because I have hoped in your word.

75   I know, O Lord, that your rules are righteous, and that in faithfulness you have afflicted me.

76   Let your steadfast love comfort me according to your promise to your servant.

77   Let your mercy come to me, that I may live; for your law is my delight.

78   Let the insolent be put to shame, because they have wronged me with falsehood; as for me, I will meditate on your precepts.

79   Let those who fear you turn to me, that they may know your testimonies.

80   May my heart be blameless in your statutes, that I may not be put to shame!

# Surgeon's Scalpel

Holy God—my architect, designer and creator—Your Word is life; You spoke Your command and created all things. I desire to live the commands You have given us by learning them and obeying them, but I am not capable of understanding them unless You enable me. It's not because Your commands are written in a language I don't know; it's because my selfish heart and polluted mind refuse to recognize Your authority. Therefore, I confess that my only hope rests in Your willingness to deliver me; Your Word must deliver me from myself.

You open my eyes to areas of hidden sin, and Your Spirit convicts me of my rebellion. I trust Your Word to work in me, flushing out these tatters of my old nature, cutting them away from my life, and replacing them with the fruit of Your Spirit. No matter how painful I find the process, I know it is the Surgeon's scalpel employed in mercy and steadfast love.

As my incisions heal, I find You are replacing my wreck of a life with the beauty of my life's original design bathed in Your glory. The joy and peace that radiate from me attract those who worship You. They rejoice with me and praise You as they see Your life flowing through me. Thank You for restoring me and displaying the beauty You always meant for me to have.

Lord, let Your life radiate from me so brightly that those who wrong me will be shamed. Just as I saw myself in Your Word and recognized my rebellion, do the same in them. I wronged others, but You forgave me. Bring this same repentance to those who wrong me when they see Your Word living in me. By Your power and mercy, make all our hearts blameless so on the day of the Lord, we will not be ashamed.

# Psalm 119:81–88 (Kaph)

81  My soul longs for your salvation; I hope in your word.

82  My eyes long for your promise; I ask, "When will you comfort me?"

83  For I have become like a wineskin in the smoke, yet I have not forgotten your statutes.

84  How long must your servant endure? When will you judge those who persecute me?

85  The insolent have dug pitfalls for me; they do not live according to your law.

86  All your commandments are sure; they persecute me with falsehood; help me!

87  They have almost made an end of me on earth, but I have not forsaken your precepts.

88  In your steadfast love give me life, that I may keep the testimonies of your mouth.

# WHEN?

When will You return, Lord Jesus? My soul yearns to be free from my sinful nature that drags me down. Every day, Your Spirit works in me to overcome the pride within and the pitfalls without. Thank You, Holy Spirit, for teaching me, guiding me, and protecting me. I fight on simply because You strengthen me, but I nevertheless grow weary. Jesus, my eyes ache with longing to see Your promised return.

I trust Your Word. In it I find daily encouragement to continue in patient endurance. As I endure, I study, learn, and practice Your ways. I am changing into the person You designed me to be. Nevertheless, I battle my sin-nature every day. I've become a weary warrior who anticipates an end to all hostilities.

You won the war on the cross, Lord, but Your enemies refuse to admit defeat. They strive to keep me from sharing Your victory, placing traps and barricades before my every step. How long will You wait before You return to pronounce judgment on Your enemies?

Refresh me, Lord. Strengthen me, Holy Spirit. Evil ones work feverishly to spread their lies across the world, sensing that Your return is near. When You return, I want to be found fighting where the battle is fiercest. If I die in the fight, may my final words be, "Even so, Lord, when will You return?"

# Psalm 119:89–96 (Lamedh)

89   Forever, O Lord, your word is firmly fixed in the heavens.

90   Your faithfulness endures to all generations; you have established the earth, and it stands fast.

91   By your appointment they stand this day, for all things are your servants.

92   If your law had not been my delight, I would have perished in my affliction.

93   I will never forget your precepts, for by them you have given me life.

94   I am yours; save me, for I have sought your precepts.

95   The wicked lie in wait to destroy me, but I consider your testimonies.

96   I have seen a limit to all perfection, but your commandment is exceedingly broad.

# UNLIMITED PERFECTION

You are sovereign, Lord and so is Your Word, a firm and faithful foundation. Just as all creation serves You by continuing in its appointed places, so Your commands serve You by bringing our attention to the hostility we have toward You.

Without Your laws, I would have persisted in my wicked ways. Your Word showed me the destructive highway I traveled, illuminated the only exit, and guided me onto the path of righteousness. I found life eternal and all-encompassing love because I found You in the Bible.

Now, I delight in reading the Scriptures. Your Spirit opens the mysteries I find in the Bible's pages. I seek to know and understand Your precepts, meditating on the purposes of Your will. Your Word is Your tender compassion spelled out so everyone may see Your eagerness to have humanity—who has totally rejected You—reconciled with You.

Every object in Your universe has a limit to its perfection except Your Word. It is part of Your limitless perfection. I love creation because it displays Your glory, but I cherish Your Word because in it You show me Your love in all its boundless perfection.

# Psalm 119:97–104 (Mem)

97    Oh how I love your law! It is my meditation all the day.

98    Your commandment makes me wiser than my enemies, for it is ever with me.

99    I have more understanding than all my teachers, for your testimonies are my meditation.

100   I understand more than the aged, for I keep your precepts.

101   I hold back my feet from every evil way, in order to keep your word.

102   I do not turn aside from your rules, for you have taught me.

103   How sweet are your words to my taste, sweeter than honey to my mouth!

104   Through your precepts I get understanding; therefore I hate every false way.

# HONEY IN THE COMB

Oh, Lord, how I love Your law! I can't get enough of it. Your Word fills me with wisdom. My enemies say, "The way to God is by many paths"; however, Your Word says, "There is only one mediator between God and man—the man Christ Jesus." (1Timothy 2:5) I trusted what Your Word told me and evaded their death traps.

My teachers say, "It's all right to be sexually active with anyone as long as you both agree." You solemnly declare, "A man shall leave his father and his mother and hold fast to his wife and they shall become one flesh." (Genesis 2:24) I obey You and thus find a life that far exceeds my teachers' understanding.

The "experts" and "authorities" claim that a pregnant woman has the right to decide whether the baby growing inside her will live or die. The Bible says, "For you (God) formed my inward parts, you knitted me together in my mother's womb." (Psalm 139:13) I shudder for the callous disregard for life that these "wise ones" display. I pray for repentance and forgiveness for those believing their lies and following the evil path.

Lord, You know the ugly truth. You know I would have followed the ways of my enemies, my teachers, and the "experts" except for one thing: You taught me the truth through the Bible. I evaded evil paths, so why would it be any wonder that Your Word tastes sweet to me? I learned to recognize and hate every false way. Most of all, Your Word taught me to rely on You, to be confident in Your care of me, and to count on Your faithfulness. Oh, Lord, that makes it sweeter to me than any honey in the comb.

# Psalm 119:105-112 (Nun)

**105** Your word is a lamp to my feet and a light to my path.

**106** I have sworn an oath and confirmed it, to keep your righteous rules.

**107** I am severely afflicted; give me life, O Lord , according to your word!

**108** Accept my freewill offerings of praise, O Lord, and teach me your rules.

**109** I hold my life in my hand continually, but I do not forget your law.

**110** The wicked have laid a snare for me, but I do not stray from your precepts.

**111** Your testimonies are my heritage forever, for they are the joy of my heart.

**112** I incline my heart to perform your statutes forever, to the end.

# JOY OF MY HEART

The way of the world is a broad boulevard. Its great, wide way seeks to dazzle me with neon distractions and beckons me to walk with the crowd and choose pleasant amusements. Lord, I am tempted. I would like to try some of the distractions offered by the merchants of sin. Would it be so wrong to try some just to discover what they are like?

No, God. I will not. I resist by the power of Your Spirit. I promised You I would follow Your Way. Would I give up my place in Your family that Jesus bought for me on the cross? No way! Your laws, statutes, and commands are the breath of my life.

Lord, I don't travel on the broad boulevard with its reckless revelers and dazzling distractions; I walk the quiet, narrow path whose illumination comes only from the Bible. Sometimes, I fail to see what You mean, hardly understanding the words. Other times, Your Words speak powerfully to me. I fall on my knees to praise You, bathed in the light of Your glory.

Shortcuts tempt me to follow my own understanding, to find my own path, but I would be taking my life into my own weak hands if I did so. Lord, thank You for all the times You protected me from my bad decisions. I know from experience it is Your guidance that makes the right path clear to me.

Sometimes, I have only enough light to take the next step. I place my life in Your hands and step out. Your faithfulness sustains me as I trust in the promises I claim from Your Word. Because You gave me eternal life, You made Your Word my heritage forever. While travelers on the broad way may experience fleeting happiness, You make Your Word the joy of my heart—forever.

# Psalm 119:113-120 (Samekh)

---

113    I hate the double-minded, but I love your law.

114    You are my hiding place and my shield; I hope in your word.

115    Depart from me, you evildoers, that I may keep the commandments of my God.

116    Uphold me according to your promise, that I may live, and let me not be put to shame in my hope!

117    Hold me up, that I may be safe and have regard for your statutes continually!

118    You spurn all who go astray from your statutes, for their cunning is in vain.

119    All the wicked of the earth you discard like dross, therefore I love your testimonies.

120    My flesh trembles for fear of you, and I am afraid of your judgments.

# GOD ALONE

Lord, I find it ridiculously easy to be double minded. I say I love Your laws, but to what do I turn to obtain peace and satisfaction? Sometimes I turn to God and money or to God and love. I see others turn to God and my church or to God and my football team. Regardless of what it is we set equal to You in our hearts, we are afraid. Sometime we fear You will take it away from us. Sometimes, as we pursue that which we desire, we fear You will never give it to us.

Why am I afraid to surrender my heart's desire to You? Why do I fail to cast my hope on You alone? My reluctance to trust You mystifies me. You shield me and hide me. When I seek You in the Bible, I find hope so pure and so rich that I gladly anchor my life in You.

Holy Spirit, any time I turn to anything other than the Bible for help or hope, jerk me back to my senses. Father, give me such a passion for You that my hope will never be placed on anything less than Jesus so the source of my hope will never be a source of shame.

Father, I pray for others who hold back from following You completely. Open their eyes to the future in store for them if they remain double minded. Give them the horror of experiencing Your rejection and of being discarded with the wicked. Just so, Lord, should my love for You ever weaken, remind me of my fear of Your judgments. Cure us all of being double minded. Enable us to abandon everything and trust in You alone.

# Psalm 119:121-128 (Ayin)

---

**121** I have done what is just and right; do not leave me to my oppressors.

**122** Give your servant a pledge of good; let not the insolent oppress me.

**123** My eyes long for your salvation and for the fulfillment of your righteous promise.

**124** Deal with your servant according to your steadfast love, and teach me your statutes.

**125** I am your servant; give me understanding, that I may know your testimonies!

**126** It is time for the Lord to act, for your law has been broken.

**127** Therefore I love your commandments above gold, above fine gold.

**128** Therefore I consider all your precepts to be right; I hate every false way.

# TIME FULFILLED

You wait to act, God, until the times have been fulfilled. The Israelites lived in Egypt for four hundred years until the time of the Canaanites was over. Prophets through the centuries waited for the coming of Christ the Redeemer, but of all the prophets, only John the Baptist saw Jesus begin His ministry.

Now, the whole earth waits in fear and expectation. It is again time for You to act. You prepare us now for a season unlike any other in our experience. It will test our faith in Your goodness.

As You direct, I prepare, but I feel inadequate to correctly understand the signs of the times. I serve You with my whole heart and desire to use everything You place in my hands to meet the needs of my family and my neighbors in ways that will display Your love and glory. However, I cannot prepare against physical attack; I feel defenseless.

Already, the insolent oppress us; they seek every false way. They mock You and Your perfect law; they call evil good and live wickedly. While spiritual oppression occurs around the world, in the coming season, the physical oppression that is true in parts of the world may reach everywhere. I need You to hide me in the cleft of the rock and shelter me under Your wings. Turn my fear into faith and my anxiety into peace. Increase my trust in You to defend and protect me.

I love You, Lord, and Your commandments. I trust You to work out Your plan for me as I serve You. You are faithful to Your promises, so I meditate on Your Word. Give me understanding so I may learn Your will and pray for You to fulfill it at the appointed time.

# Psalm 119:129-136 (Pe)

129  Your testimonies are wonderful; therefore my soul keeps them.

130  The unfolding of your words gives light; it imparts understanding to the simple.

131  I open my mouth and pant, because I long for your commandments.

132  Turn to me and be gracious to me, as is your way with those who love your name.

133  Keep steady my steps according to your promise, and let no iniquity get dominion over me.

134  Redeem me from man's oppression, that I may keep your precepts.

135  Make your face shine upon your servant, and teach me your statutes.

136  My eyes shed streams of tears, because people do not keep your law.

# LIFE FOR THE SIMPLE

Lord, my heart breaks over the dreadful life of the simple. They wander through life, ignoring You. They fill their days with the work of their hands and their nights with distractions. They never ask, "Is this all there is to life?" As long as life is easy, they are satisfied.

The simple are blind to the grace You give those who love You. If only they would turn toward You and seek You in Your Word! The Bible is a wondrous, living door to Your presence; when we read it and meditate upon it, You unfold the meaning of Your Word, giving light and guidance to us.

I was once satisfied with my life, empty though it was. In Your mercy, You showed me I had no life without You. You offered to rescue me from my sinful lifestyle and to give me life in You, and I accepted.

After that event, You gave me a never-ending thirst to learn and to obey Your commands. Your Word lights my path and protects me from temptation and fear. Your Spirit teaches me ways to serve You. I know joy in Your presence because of Your Word.

The simple know nothing of this, Lord, and so my heart breaks. I cry because they ignore You, becoming fools in the end. Unless, Lord ... yes, unless You do for them what You did for me. Make them dissatisfied with who they are. Shine the light of Your love and mercy upon them. As only You can do, give life to the simple so they become Your faithful children.

# Psalm 119:137-144 (Tsadhe)

---

**137**   Righteous are you, O Lord, and right are your rules.

**138**   You have appointed your testimonies in righteousness and in all faithfulness.

**139**   My zeal consumes me, because my foes forget your words.

**140**   Your promise is well tried, and your servant loves it.

**141**   I am small and despised, yet I do not forget your precepts.

**142**   Your righteousness is righteous forever, and your law is true.

**143**   Trouble and anguish have found me out, but your commandments are my delight.

**144**   Your testimonies are righteous forever; give me understanding that I may live.

# HEARTS WHO LOVE YOUR WORD

My God, what can I do? My anger and frustration overwhelm me.

I love the Bible. I escape from the boundaries of time when I sit in Your presence and study the Scriptures. I find jewels of righteousness and gems of faith. In my eagerness to share this immeasurable treasure, I talk to my friends. My excitement bores the ones who do not know You. "That's all right for you, but I don't need it," they tell me as they walk away. My Christian friends eye me with confusion. "So what's the big deal?" they ask. "That's old news." Then they change the subject.

*Okay*, I think. *I'll tell the pastor. He will understand my excitement.* When I tried to tell of Your words that had touched my heart, Lord, he didn't really listen. When I left him, I felt insignificant and ignored.

Lord, I need to share Your promises and precepts with someone who understands and rejoices with me. Your words burn in me. Is there no one who loves You and delights to talk about Your Word? Send me brothers and sisters whose hearts love Your Word and whose lifestyles show evidence of their obedience to Your leading.

As You send them, bind our hearts in our love for Your Word. Make it alive for us and in us as we delight in it. Help us to encourage each other in proclaiming Your truth. Give us a passion for sharing Your Word with those who don't know You. When we meet those who reject Your truth, give us the endurance to continue. In the Bible, we find life to share and courage to pass it on. Strengthen us to spread the good news that Your will and Your way are righteous forever.

# Psalm 119:145-152 (Qoph)

---

**145** With my whole heart I cry; answer me, O Lord! I will keep your statutes.

**146** I call to you; save me, that I may observe your testimonies.

**147** I rise before dawn and cry for help; I hope in your words.

**148** My eyes are awake before the watches of the night, that I may meditate on your promise.

**149** Hear my voice according to your steadfast love; O Lord, according to your justice give me life.

**150** They draw near who persecute me with evil purpose; they are far from your law.

**151** But you are near, O Lord, and all your commandments are true.

**152** Long have I known from your testimonies that you have founded them forever.

# Long Ago, Far Away

In distress of soul, I focus my entire being on You, passionately calling, "Save me, Lord, save me so I may seek and follow Your decrees."

Long ago, I learned that the words in the Bible apply to me. All those who wrote them are dead; their bones have turned to dust. Nevertheless, Your Word lives on, promising me forgiveness and eternal life. I get up early and stay up late to study the Scriptures in which I find Your steadfast love and everlasting promises.

I meditate on Your promises, God. They connect me to You and commit You to caring for me. What a comfort they are when I am distressed. Those who live far away from Your Word have no such comfort. They rebel, persecute, and scorn; they act without pity and live without love. They commit to nothing and no one except to lives guided only by their selfish desires.

As I trust You to fulfill Your promises, I commit myself to following You and obeying Your commands. You promise blessings to Your faithful ones. You commit all You are to those who put their trust in You.

I come into Your presence, Father, because Jesus is not only my Savior but also the One who has authority over me. I wait here for Your command. If my commitment wavers, Holy Spirit, remind me that my imperfect obedience is no reason to desert my commitment to You. You made Your commitment with absolute power. As I consent to obey You and cooperate with Your plan for me, You hold me firmly in place. Thank You.

The reasons for my distress come and go, but Your promises are always with me. I commit to obeying You with my whole heart. Lead me, Lord. I listen for Your Word to guide me on Your path through these distressing times. The Bible may have been written long ago, but it is never far away from my heart.

# Psalm 119:153-160 (Resh)

---

**153**  Look on my affliction and deliver me, for I do not forget your law.

**154**  Plead my cause and redeem me; give me life according to your promise!

**155**  Salvation is far from the wicked, for they do not seek your statutes.

**156**  Great is your mercy, O Lord; give me life according to your rules.

**157**  Many are my persecutors and my adversaries, but I do not swerve from your testimonies.

**158**  I look at the faithless with disgust, because they do not keep your commands.

**159**  Consider how I love your precepts! Give me life according to your steadfast love.

**160**  The sum of your word is truth, and every one of your righteous rules endures forever.

# You Give Me Life

Lord, how I treasure Your Word. When affliction overwhelms me, the Holy Spirit reminds me of Your instructions, "Trust in the Lord with all your heart and do not lean on your own understanding (Proverbs 3:5).

Jesus, I love the Bible because it tells me the history of Your redeeming sacrifice on the cross. I rejoice in the picture of Your love it displays. I take comfort and courage knowing through the Bible that You are interceding for me right now in heaven. Thank You for always being *for* me.

Your Word is so precious to me that I grieve for those who want a Bible but cannot get one. The wicked who could easily read a Bible but who refuse endanger themselves. When they become adversaries of Your children and persecute us, You hold them doubly responsible for their actions.

Because Your Word says I do not battle against people but against spiritual opponents, I keep my eyes on You. You guide me and strengthen me as I fight the battle of faith. Your eternal Word is my life support and my light. Fill me with the kind of life that comes only from You so everyone who sees me may praise You.

# Psalm 119:161-168 (Sin and Shin)

161  Princes persecute me without cause, but my heart stands in awe of your words.

162  I rejoice at your word like one who finds great spoil.

163  I hate and abhor falsehood, but I love your law.

164  Seven times a day I praise you for your righteous rules.

165  Great peace have those who love your law; nothing can make them stumble.

166  I hope for your salvation, O Lord, and I do your commandments.

167  My soul keeps your testimonies; I love them exceedingly.

168  I keep your precepts and testimonies, for all my ways are before you.

# Our Hearts in Awe

Lord, I am not a brave person, so when someone challenges me, I usually retreat. Nevertheless, I have found one experience in which Your Spirit gives me courage to stand—when someone who claims to be an authority pours mockery and scorn on Your Word.

My heart stands in awe of Your Word. The Bible is beauty, purity, and truth, so why do the wicked persist in twisting its words? They mutilate beauty, defile purity, and poison truth. I abhor the tormented lies Your Word becomes in the mouths of some "experts."

Your Word deserves for me to take a stand, to proclaim it rightly. I read Your Word every day. Each time it speaks to me; I find living words. I have abundant reasons to thank You for the many ways You speak through Your Word.

All my ways are an open book before You. You know what I need to take a stand. Give me wisdom and courage to speak out at just the right time. Let Your Spirit saturate me with peace, and give me words filled with Your power; only then can my defense of Your Word strike the hearts of the listeners and keep us all from stumbling.

Let Your enemies keep silent because Your Word is true. Protect the wandering sheep from becoming the enemies' spoil. Instead, lead us all to stand—with our hearts in awe—before You.

# Psalm 119:169-176 (Taw)

---

**169** Let my cry come before you, O Lord; give me understanding according to your word!

**170** Let my plea come before you; deliver me according to your word.

**171** My lips will pour forth praise, for you teach me your statutes.

**172** My tongue will sing of your word, for all your commandments are right.

**173** Let your hand be ready to help me, for I have chosen your precepts.

**174** I long for your salvation, O Lord, and your law is my delight.

**175** Let my soul live and praise you, and let your rules help me.

**176** I have gone astray like a lost sheep; seek your servant, for I do not forget your commandments.

# YOUR ETERNAL WORD

I love the Bible, Lord. Your Word delights me. Every word displays truth, light, and love. Without it, my life would be barren. Nevertheless, Your Word also distresses me. I see perfection in Your laws—laws I break too easily. I need You to teach me Your way and deliver me from my sinful paths. Deliver me based on Your love and mercy, because no matter how many of Your laws I keep, I disobey others.

Father, I long for You to complete my salvation that began when I accepted Jesus as my Savior. I know that when I live in heaven, sin will no longer pollute my obedience. Now, I stray from Your Word so easily, like a clueless sheep wandering off into the wilderness. In spite of my occasional wayward wanderings, I want to follow Your plans for me. I trust You to move my heart and return me to Your path when I stray.

When I complete my assignment here and dwell with You in heaven, my soul will live in praise of Your Word. For now, my lips praise it. I find new reasons every day to thank You for the Bible. My tongue sings of my delight in finding You within its pages. In heaven, I will find new pleasure in Your Word; it will be even more glorious there. In heaven, I will be free to obey all Your commands. Yes, in heaven, I will find fresh reasons to praise the glory of Your Word forever.

# PSALM 120

1    In my distress I called to the Lord, and he answered me.

2    Deliver me, O Lord, from lying lips, from a deceitful tongue.

3    What shall be given to you, and what more shall be done to you, you deceitful tongue?

4    A warrior's sharp arrows, with glowing coals of the broom tree!

5    Woe to me, that I sojourn in Meshech, that I dwell among the tents of Kedar!

6    Too long have I had my dwelling among those who hate peace.

7    I am for peace, but when I speak, they are for war!

# Lying Lips, Deceitful Tongues

Why do some people hate peace, Lord? They sow discord in all their relationships. Like speedboats leaving roiling wakes behind them, they leave trails of turmoil wherever they go. Peace is elusive enough in this sinful world, so why do they spend all their strength opposing it?

Physical violence afflicts those who can least resist it. Lord, protect the battered women, the abused children, and the suffering elderly. Keep them out of the control of those who enjoy causing pain in others.

More prevalent, however, than physical abusers are those with deceitful tongues. Those who destroy with their tongues live everywhere. Some people lie to avoid rebuke or punishment, while other people seek personal profit in deceiving others. Most common are those who spread vicious lies and malicious rumors just to stir people's emotions and destroy peace. All liars seek to inflict their selfishness on others. Cleanse their hearts with the fire of truth, Lord. Let the damage they meant to inflict on others rebound on them. Show them the consequences of their deceit.

I live as a foreigner in the land of the lost—Your ambassador of peace. Guide me, Lord, to spread Your peace, not just the temporary pause of hostilities the world calls peace. Use me to radiate Your love and peace in ways that draw people to You. Only in You can we find the purity of truth and the contentment of peace.

# Psalm 121

1    I lift up my eyes to the hills. From where does my help come?

2    My help comes from the Lord, who made heaven and earth.

3    He will not let your foot be moved; he who keeps you will not slumber.

4    Behold, he who keeps Israel will neither slumber nor sleep.

5    The Lord is your keeper; the Lord is your shade on your right hand.

6    The sun shall not strike you by day, nor the moon by night.

7    The Lord will keep you from all evil; he will keep your life.

8    The Lord will keep your going out and your coming in from this time forth and forevermore.

# THE DAYS AT THE END

Yes, I lift my eyes to You, Lord. Today, that is all I can lift. My strength deserted me, leaving a heavy weight of weakness. My heart pounds with the least exertion, and I pant for breath.

How did I come to this, Lord? For years, vigor, strength, and energy fueled my days. At night, my exhaustion came from a day well spent performing satisfying work. Then, one day, I awoke to discover things formerly accomplished without conscious thought started requiring concentration and considerable effort. My body weakened with age. Where once I cared for myself and helped others, I found myself needing someone else to care for me. Lord, sometimes I feel ashamed to be so dependent.

What can I do? I can lift my eyes up to You. I have experienced Your faithful care all my life. I depend on You to protect me from falling as I stumble along. I remember that You never sleep when I lie awake in the night; you keep me company in the darkness.

Even more than in the past, I need You to keep me safe. Shelter me from harm day and night. Protect me from evil people who want to take advantage of me. Hide my life in the cleft of the rock. You numbered my days from my first coming in; order my days to my last going out. You, who made me, will lovingly care for me to the end of my days. I will lift my eyes and praise You.

# Psalm 122

1     I was glad when they said to me, "Let us go to the house of the Lord!"

2     Our feet have been standing within your gates, O Jerusalem!

3     Jerusalem—built as a city that is bound firmly together,

4     to which the tribes go up, the tribes of the Lord, as was decreed for Israel, to give thanks to the name of the Lord.

5     There thrones for judgment were set, the thrones of the house of David.

6     Pray for the peace of Jerusalem! "May they be secure who love you!

7     Peace be within your walls and security within your towers!"

8     For my brothers and companions' sake I will say, "Peace be within you!"

9     For the sake of the house of the Lord our God, I will seek your good.

# CITY OF PEACE?

Father, do You ever tire of all my questions because I understand so little of Your Word? I come with another one. Why Jerusalem, Lord? What has Jerusalem ever done to deserve the title "City of God?" Its citizens killed Your prophets when they didn't want to hear Your message. With Roman help, they crucified Jesus. They persecuted anyone who confessed Jesus as Messiah. Still today, they follow false gods—pride, lust, and independence from You.

Nevertheless, You chose Jerusalem as the Holy City. From it, You blessed us with the Words of life, the resurrection of Jesus, and, through the Holy Spirit, the birth of the church. Your love for the city is so great that You command us to pray for its peace.

Jerusalem has seen no peace in the last sixty years, but by faith, we bless Jerusalem as we pray, "God bring peace within her walls and security for all she protects." We confidently expect You to answer our prayer since we know the Prince of Peace will return to this city.

Lord Jesus, You tell us in Your Word that the mountain where Jerusalem sits will one day tower over all the earth. You will sit on the throne of David to condemn sin and death. You, the Prince of Peace, will make Jerusalem the City of Peace.

Because You love Jerusalem, I will pray for the city's peace. Because I love You and eagerly await Your return, I will seek Jerusalem's welfare.

# Psalm 123

1    To you I lift up my eyes, O you who are enthroned in the heavens!

2    Behold, as the eyes of servants look to the hand of their master, as the eyes of a maidservant to the hand of her mistress, so our eyes look to the Lord our God, till he has mercy upon us.

3    Have mercy upon us, O Lord, have mercy upon us, for we have had more than enough of contempt.

4    Our soul has had more than enough of the scorn of those who are at ease, of the contempt of the proud.

# MUTE MISERY

Oh Lord, my God, I cry out to You for mercy. I plead before Your throne, bowed down with wrenching grief. I grieve because rampant evil shapes our nation. One lash at a time, we are scourged by our legal system as it strips away our national dependence on You. We who stand firmly on the laws set forth in Your Word feel increasingly isolated. We have no excuse for leaving our godly heritage. I look to You in mute misery.

Yes, I lift my eyes to You, my God. Our deliverance comes from no one else. Only You, who are enthroned in heaven, can alter the river of history in its making. Only You can channel a nation's will to live as one nation under God.

I will fix my eyes upon You, day and night, eager to see the release of the first drops of mercy. I will wait for showers of mercy to soften hearts. I will plead for the storms of mercy that call for national repentance. I will rejoice to see the scorn of the rich and powerful silenced and the contempt of the proud turned to shame.

Only Your omnipotent power can deliver me from my misery, so I fall on my face before You. I lie quiet and expectant, like a slave before a king. I await Your decision, confident I can trust You to be merciful.

# Psalm 124

1     If it had not been the Lord who was on our side—let Israel now say—

2     if it had not been the Lord who was on our side when people rose up against us,

3     then they would have swallowed us up alive, when their anger was kindled against us;

4     then the flood would have swept us away, the torrent would have gone over us;

5     then over us would have gone the raging waters.

6     Blessed be the Lord, who has not given us as prey to their teeth!

7     We have escaped like a bird from the snare of the fowlers; the snare is broken, and we have escaped!

8     Our help is in the name of the Lord, who made heaven and earth.

# "But God ..."

Wow, God, that was a narrow escape. That car zoomed past me so close that I could have reached out the window and slapped it. It seemed to come out of nowhere. Fear turned my skin cold and closed my throat. My heart raced almost at the speed of those disappearing taillights. Everyone in the car could have been killed.

"But God ..."

I love that phrase, Father. Anything that follows, "but God ..." You bathe in love, tender care, and gentle mercy. It speaks to me of times You interrupt the schemes of men or devils to harm me. It tells me You watch over me night and day and all Your plans for me are good. Best of all, that phrase tells me that You—not those who cause chaos—control even the smallest details of my life.

Yes, when I feel trapped by circumstances or paralyzed by events, I remember, "but God ..." and turn to You. Even when life becomes cruel and heartless in evil times, I wrap myself in the comfort that You are on my side. My trials may be severe, but they will only drive me to my knees to confess my faith in Your plan to deliver me. You are my God; my help comes from You.

# Psalm 125

1  Those who trust in the Lord are like Mount Zion, which cannot be moved, but abides forever.

2  As the mountains surround Jerusalem, so the Lord surrounds his people, from this time forth and forevermore.

3  For the scepter of wickedness shall not rest on the land allotted to the righteous, lest the righteous stretch out their hands to do wrong.

4  Do good, O Lord, to those who are good, and to those who are upright in their hearts!

5  But those who turn aside to their crooked ways the Lord will lead away with evildoers! Peace be upon Israel!

# MOUNTAIN OF THE LORD

Lord, Your Word tells us that in the age to come, all the islands will disappear and the mountains will fall—except for one: Mount Zion, the mountain of the Lord. At that time, You will shake everything that can be shaken, but Mount Zion will stand firm.

Father, in this age, You shake the world every day. Uncertainty glares in the daylight, and fears blaze in the night. Illness claims the old, and wars cut off the young. Illusions shatter, and expectations implode. Safety is a mirage, and security is but a broken promise. Where can I turn except to You, Lord?

My hope is fixed on You. You are my heart's desire. You alone are my peace in chaos, my comfort in deep grief, and my hope when everything fails.

This world's shaking may wipe out my wealth, destroy my home, or claim those I love, but it cannot shake my confidence in You, the creator of Mount Zion. Evil rulers may claim temporary ownership of Mount Zion, but they cannot move Your mountain. Their crooked ways will lead them to their rightful punishment.

Because I trust in You, You will go before me and behind me, protecting me from taking up crooked ways. I will never be moved; I will abide in You forever on the Mountain of the Lord.

# PSALM 126

1     When the Lord restored the fortunes of Zion, we were like those who dream.

2     Then our mouth was filled with laughter, and our tongue with shouts of joy; then they said among the nations, "The Lord has done great things for them."

3     The Lord has done great things for us; we are glad.

4     Restore our fortunes, O Lord, like streams in the Negeb!

5     Those who sow in tears shall reap with shouts of joy!

6     He who goes out weeping, bearing the seed for sowing, shall come home with shouts of joy, bringing his sheaves with him.

# Tears of Desperation

Lord, the history of Your church overflows with stories of backsliding and restoration. Many times, despair closed in around us only to be melted away by the power of Your Spirit poured out on us. We have learned we can trust You to faithfully see us through to victory.

Father, our need is greater now than in the past. The American part of Your church suffers from a devastating drought much more harmful than physical drought. The rain I seek is not one of water but of Your Spirit.

On my face before You, I confess that our American church is made up of dry bones; it has a form but not the substance of godliness. Our lips may praise You in places for worship, but our hearts are far from You. We cannot make disciples of others because we are not ourselves disciples. We are cultural Christians—the worst of hypocrites. Forgive, Lord!

Praise You, God and Father of our Lord, Jesus Christ! Our condition is not hopeless. You crucified Jesus and raised Him from death to restore us. Restore us, O Lord.

You do not change between one generation and another; You poured out Your Spirit to restore Your church before, and You will do so again. Has any part of Your church of any generation in any nation needed Your restoration as much as we need it now? We fall before You with tears of desperation because our need is overwhelming.

Open our ears to hear Your call to "Follow Me." Fill our hearts with a passion to plant the seed of Your Word, first in our own lives and then in others. Work the miracle of life and growth in our hearts' fertile fields. Give us plentiful harvests of hearts returned to You, of godly lives and of faithful service. Oh, Lord, do not leave us in this desperate state but bring us back with shouts of joy. Restore us, Lord.

# Psalm 127

1  Unless the Lord builds the house, those who build it labor in vain. Unless the Lord watches over the city, the watchman stays awake in vain.

2  It is in vain that you rise up early and go late to rest, eating the bread of anxious toil; for he gives to his beloved sleep.

3  Behold, children are a heritage from the Lord the fruit of the womb a reward.

4  Like arrows in the hand of a warrior are the children of one's youth.

5  Blessed is the man who fills his quiver with them! He shall not be put to shame when he speaks with his enemies in the gate.

# SOLOMON'S WISDOM

Lord, I sometimes think that Solomon—in spite of all You gave him—needed an attitude adjustment. He began writing Ecclesiastes with "Vanity of vanities … all is vanity." Here he is again in this psalm, writing about life's activities performed in vain.

Solomon was obviously a "glass half empty" person. He was right, of course. Unless You build the house, protect the city, and bless the laborer, all humanity works in vain. I still think he missed the point.

Didn't Solomon ever enjoy the experience of working on a house You built? What about the temple? Solomon's temple was the richest, most beautiful house of worship ever built for Your glory. Did he never feel the joy and amazement that should have been his as Your plans took form?

You gave Solomon not just one city but also Israel, a most expansive kingdom over which to rule. He had state-of-the-art weapons, treaties with neighboring kingdoms, and Your promises of peace and protection. Did he never feel at peace? Was he always insecure while ruling Israel?

At least Solomon acknowledged that his children were gifts from You, but even in this matter, he spoke of their benefit to himself. He described his grown sons as weapons kept near in the presence of his enemies; he felt less intimidated with his sons at his side.

Lord, give me Your wisdom that I might live my life for Your honor and glory. I also ask for the ability to rejoice in all Your creation as I work and to delight in my children as they mature. I desire to live with thanksgiving—a glass always overflowing with gratitude.

# Psalm 128

1    Blessed is everyone who fears the Lord, who walks in his ways!

2    You shall eat the fruit of the labor of your hands; you shall be blessed, and it shall be well with you.

3    Your wife will be like a fruitful vine within your house; your children will be like olive shoots around your table.

4    Behold, thus shall the man be blessed who fears the Lord.

5    The Lord bless you from Zion! May you see the prosperity of Jerusalem all the days of your life!

6    May you see your children's children! Peace be upon Israel!

# GODLY MEN

Father, You seek godly men. While our culture values young, handsome, virile men, You want promise keepers. As the vigor of youth declines, we idolize power, wealth, and position, while You yearn for kingdom men. You desire men who repent of their sins and are reconciled with You by the sacrifice of Jesus.

Father, call out those men who will accept Jesus as Lord and Savior to live daily in awe of You. Challenge men to lead and serve their families without counting the costs. Guide men through rocky rapids of immaturity, self-seeking, and midlife crises. Lead them into the deep currents of maturity, selfless service, and walking in Your way.

Because godly sons, promise keepers, and kingdom men obey You with committed hearts and loving hands, You bless them with wonderful promises: wives who bring joy to their homes, energetic children who show great potential, and profit from the work of their hands. The blessings You give to godly men multiply and produce blessings of prosperity and security for the whole family.

Please lead godly men to disciple other men and their sons in Your ways, strengthening their cities, building them up, and making them prosper. Lord, one man, one husband, one father at a time, You change whole communities. Shape our hearts and guide our prayers to intercede for all the men we know to become godly men.

# Psalm 129

1     "Greatly have they afflicted me from my youth"—let Israel now say—

2     "Greatly have they afflicted me from my youth, yet they have not prevailed against me.

3     The plowers plowed upon my back; they made long their furrows."

4     The Lord is righteous; he has cut the cords of the wicked.

5     May all who hate Zion be put to shame and turned backward!

6     Let them be like the grass on the housetops, which withers before it grows up,

7     with which the reaper does not fill his hand nor the binder of sheaves his arms,

8     nor do those who pass by say, "The blessing of the Lord be upon you! We bless you in the name of the Lord!"

# School of Consequences

Lord, You called me into Your family when I was only a child. You designed my life so I would be a vessel of honor. In my youth, however, I made sinful choices, turning aside from Your laws. I chose the tools to mold me instead of allowing You to choose them. The ones I chose caused me many years of great affliction and terrible trials. I had chosen to study at the school of consequences.

Years after You had cut the cords of pain, I could finally see Your hands at work in that school. Events that caused me physical pain protected me from degrading experiences. Trials that brought me emotional distress guarded me from altogether deserting You. In the school of consequences, I learned that I was helpless without You and dependent on You for light and life.

As a graduate, I see that those who attended with me and claimed to be my friends but hated You were my enemies too. When I refused to join their ceaseless parties, they shunned me. I was not shamed because You comforted me. These "friends" rejected Your call and refused Your blessing and disappeared into withered, useless lives as a result.

You, O God, are sovereign. You chose me before the foundation of the world. Even though I chose the school of consequences, it failed to cripple me. You used it to mold me into a vessel of honor. I am Your child, designed to give You glory and to radiate Your life in a vessel of clay.

# Psalm 130

1   Out of the depths I cry to you, O Lord!

2   O Lord, hear my voice! Let your ears be attentive to the voice of my pleas for mercy!

3   If you, O Lord, should mark iniquities, O Lord, who could stand?

4   But with you there is forgiveness, that you may be feared.

5   I wait for the Lord, my soul waits, and in his word I hope;

6   my soul waits for the Lord more than watchmen for the morning, more than watchmen for the morning.

7   O Israel, hope in the Lord! For with the Lord there is steadfast love, and with him is plentiful redemption.

8   And he will redeem Israel from all his iniquities.

# BECAUSE OF YOUR MERCY

Lord, I always need Your mercy. The scar tissue of my rebellion cuts through the center of my human nature. Until the day death removes the last rags of my sinfulness, I will cry out for Your mercy.

Your great mercy enables me to find forgiveness for my wickedness; poured out as forgiveness, it fills me with the courage to worship and serve You. I can approach You with awe and loving reverence.

Oh Father, Your mercy displayed in explosions of steadfast love inspires me to trust only and wholly in You. It births within me a thirst to know You better, and it sends me to Your Word.

My Jesus, what love for me I find in You! Every word of Yours in the Bible warms my heart and builds my faith. You love me. You became a man for me and died for my sins. You arose from death and ascended into heaven, where You intercede for me every day.

Because of Your great mercy, my soul waits for Your return, Lord. The great and terrible day of the Lord will dawn with judgment. Nevertheless, because of Your mercy, that day brings me only the joy of completed redemption. I am shaped by Your mercy forever.

# Psalm 131

1      O Lord, my heart is not lifted up; my eyes are not raised too high;
I do not occupy myself with things too great and too marvelous
for me.

2      But I have calmed and quieted my soul, like a weaned child with
its mother; like a weaned child is my soul within me.

3      O Israel, hope in the Lord from this time forth and forevermore.

# In Your Presence Is Peace

Many times, my prayers consisted of demands: "Change these circumstances, Lord! Why are You doing this to me?" My hurting heart brought my arrogance to You. I lifted my pride-filled eyes to demand explanations, but Your love covered my sinful attitudes. You answered my prayers with what I needed, not what I wanted. You changed me.

I still do not understand the reasons You allowed certain events and people into my life; Your plans are too great for me to understand. Like Job, I am learning that as I trust You more and know better who You are, I am satisfied with not knowing.

Today, I come to You demanding nothing. I come quietly, listening, my mind and heart hungry to be in Your presence. I bow before You with no agenda. The world around me tosses in the winds of adversity, but here is peace. With heights of joy and depths of love, I worship You.

As I leave our quiet time together and take up my daily activities, I live the small role You have given me in Your great story. This tranquility of heart I take from Your presence and into the turmoil of living. I declare with my life that You are trustworthy and that my hope is in You.

# Psalm 132

1   Remember, O Lord, in David's favor, all the hardships he endured,

2   how he swore to the Lord and vowed to the Mighty One of Jacob,

3   "I will not enter my house or get into my bed,

4   I will not give sleep to my eyes or slumber to my eyelids,

5   until I find a place for the Lord, a dwelling place for the Mighty One of Jacob."

6   Behold, we heard of it in Ephrathah; we found it in the fields of Jaar.

7   "Let us go to his dwelling place; let us worship at his footstool!"

8   Arise, O Lord, and go to your resting place, you and the ark of your might.

9   Let your priests be clothed with righteousness, and let your saints shout for joy.

10  For the sake of your servant David, do not turn away the face of your anointed one.

11  The Lord swore to David a sure oath from which he will not turn back: "One of the sons of your body I will set on your throne.

12  If your sons keep my covenant and my testimonies that I shall teach them, their sons also forever shall sit on your throne."

13  For the Lord has chosen Zion; he has desired it for his dwelling place:

14  "This is my resting place forever; here I will dwell, for I have desired it.

15  I will abundantly bless her provisions; I will satisfy her poor with bread.

# Can One Man Shape the World?

Lord, You certainly tested David through his hardships. Someone always opposed him. Lions and bears stalked his sheep, and Goliath threatened to make slaves of his brothers. King Saul envied David's popularity and attempted to kill him. The Philistines fought to weaken David's kingdom and control the land. His sons plotted to steal his crown.

Your Word records his anger, frustrations, disappointments, and pain, but David did not become a bitter, rebellious man. His heart was plain to see. When, as king, he established his capital city, he sought a home for You and desired to transform the tents of Your tabernacle into a magnificent temple.

You denied him the pleasure of building it because You had called him to be a warrior. Nevertheless, You honored his passionate desire to see You worshipped above any king. You promised him a son to sit on his throne. You gave him Solomon, who built the temple. You chose Mount Zion, where David established his reign, as Your home forever. You told him that even if his grandsons failed to keep Your covenant and lost their right to sit on his throne, You would crown Your Anointed One from his lineage for his throne.

You kept that greatest promise in Jesus Christ, son of David, Son of God. In Him, You satisfy the poor with the Bread of Life, You clothe the righteous in the white linen of salvation, and You delight Your saints with shouts of joy in everlasting life. David's life ripples down the centuries to my family and me because You chose David and he loved You.

16    Her priests I will clothe with salvation, and her saints will shout for joy.

17    There I will make a horn to sprout for David; I have prepared a lamp for my anointed.

18    His enemies I will clothe with shame, but on him his crown will shine."

# My Prayer

_____

_____

_____

_____

_____

_____

_____

_____

_____

_____

_____

_____

_____

_____

_____

_____

_____

_____

_____

_____

_____

# Psalm 133

1    Behold, how good and pleasant it is when brothers dwell in unity!

2    It is like the precious oil on the head, running down on the beard, on the beard of Aaron, running down on the collar of his robes!

3    It is like the dew of Hermon, which falls on the mountains of Zion! For there the Lord has commanded the blessing, life forevermore.

# Unity's Blessing

Thank You, Father, for planting us in a church that declares that You are Almighty God, Jesus is Savior and Lord, and the Holy Spirit lives in us. We are brothers and sisters dwelling in unity to bring souls into Your kingdom and to see lives transformed.

What a blessing that unity is! Your Spirit, working to overcome our arguments, disputes, and pride is much in evidence. Even those most dedicated to Your service can be hurt by their brothers and sisters. When we live out our concern for each other and forgive both faults and slights, we honor You.

Remind us that we, like the priests at the temple, are consecrated to You. Keep us united in our worship, and focus our attention on working out Your plan for our church. Each member has a place of service in the church's activities. Some serve by leading the congregation, while others build relationships in community activities. Others clean, cook, or care for babies in the nursery. Many pray, travel on mission trips, and give financially; they undertake whatever task You've given them. In all these things, we worship You.

The members of our congregation are like plants on the mountainsides that collect the morning dew. We gather the living water and satisfy the thirst of those who want abundant life in You. You multiply the number of people who join to worship You. We are a green and fruitful place, and You bless our unity for Your Name's sake. Thank You, Lord.

# Psalm 134

1     Come, bless the Lord, all you servants of the Lord, who stand by night in the house of the Lord!

2     Lift up your hands to the holy place and bless the Lord!

3     May the Lord bless you from Zion, he who made heaven and earth!

# Good Night

Night covers the land; the struggle of living and the stress of work are restrained. The house quiets as those in the family find their beds. I come, as I did at the dawn of this day, into Your presence. One by one, I examine the events of the day. I see Your hand guiding, encouraging, directing, inspiring, and protecting. Thank You for keeping me calm in the chaos, whole in the pain, and peaceful in times of strong emotion.

Bowed here, before Your throne, I worship You. I praise You for the opportunities You gave me today to be Your hands, feet, and love as I served those who traveled with me this day. My desire is to be Your faithful servant.

My weary mind and tired body relax in Your presence. Please restore the energy I used, and give me new strength to serve You and my family tomorrow. I release all my burdens and grief to You. I trust You, the maker of heaven and earth, to faithfully care for all I love, for You love them too.

Good night, Father. I love You.

# Psalm 135

1   Praise the Lord! Praise the name of the Lord, give praise, O servants of the Lord,

2   who stand in the house of the Lord, in the courts of the house of our God!

3   Praise the Lord, for the Lord is good; sing to his name, for it is pleasant!

4   For the Lord has chosen Jacob for himself, Israel as his own possession.

5   For I know that the Lord is great, and that our Lord is above all gods.

6   Whatever the Lord pleases, he does, in heaven and on earth, in the seas and all deeps.

7   He it is who makes the clouds rise at the end of the earth, who makes lightnings for the rain and brings forth the wind from his storehouses.

8   He it was who struck down the firstborn of Egypt, both of man and of beast;

9   who in your midst, O Egypt, sent signs and wonders against Pharaoh and all his servants;

10  who struck down many nations and killed mighty kings,

11  Sihon, king of the Amorites, and Og, king of Bashan, and all the kingdoms of Canaan,

12  and gave their land as a heritage, a heritage to his people Israel.

13  Your name, O Lord, endures forever, your renown, O Lord, throughout all ages.

14  For the Lord will vindicate his people and have compassion on his servants.

# YOUR NAME

Father, our concept of You is so pathetic. We casually assert that You are God the Creator, King of all kings, Lord over every other kind of lord, but that comes from a surface knowledge, a parroting of words someone told us about You.

Where is our reverence for Your Name? We write "OMG" and turn Your Name into an exclamation of fake surprise. We say, "God bless!" in a manner that makes it a curse. That we use Your Name so callously shames me.

Lord, teach us the significance of Your Name and fill us with the reverence and respect rightfully due You. The priests in the temple and the Levites who served there praised Your Name but would neither speak nor write it because it was holy. They encouraged all who worshipped in the temple to sing *to* Your Name. They had learned that Your Name expressed Your presence in the temple with them.

Centuries later, we need not be in a place of worship to have You present. We bear Your Name—Christian—because we have Christ in us, the hope of glory. We have so much more reason to praise Your Name with our lives than did the ancient Israelites.

Sadly, Lord, our lives do not reflect this truth. Our lives display no recognition of our responsibility to live up to Your Name. We act as if You are arbitrary and unjust. You are God, ordering events according to *Your* plan. You judge Your enemies, punish the unrighteous, and dispose of kingdoms according to Your decrees. We cannot begin to understand Your purpose, so our contempt for Your Name as we judge Your actions is disgraceful.

You designed us so we would become like the god we worship. If those who worship an idol become like the idol, should we not highly regard the Name of the One God, since You desire that we become like You? Should we not delight in Your Name? It endures forever; it is remembered throughout the ages. It is the Name of Him whose image we bear.

Oh, Lord God Almighty, flood our hearts and minds with a reverent awe for Your Name, which is a strong tower for those who worship You. Grow in us such a height of respect and such a depth of trust that our lips and lives will speak well of Your Name. May all we are and everything we do praise Your Name.

15   The idols of the nations are silver and gold, the work of human hands.

16   They have mouths, but do not speak; they have eyes, but do not see;

17   they have ears, but do not hear, nor is there any breath in their mouths.

18   Those who make them become like them, so do all who trust in them!

19   O house of Israel, bless the Lord! O house of Aaron, bless the Lord!

20   O house of Levi, bless the Lord! You who fear the Lord, bless the Lord!

21   Blessed be the Lord from Zion, he who dwells in Jerusalem! Praise the Lord!

# My Prayer

_____

_____

_____

_____

_____

_____

_____

_____

_____

_____

_____

_____

_____

_____

_____

_____

_____

_____

_____

_____

_____

# Psalm 136

1   Give thanks to the Lord, for he is good, for his steadfast love endures forever.

2   Give thanks to the God of gods, for his steadfast love endures forever.

3   Give thanks to the Lord of lords, for his steadfast love endures forever;

4   to him who alone does great wonders, for his steadfast love endures forever;

5   to him who by understanding made the heavens, for his steadfast love endures forever;

6   to him who spread out the earth above the waters, for his steadfast love endures forever;

7   to him who made the great lights, for his steadfast love endures forever;

8   the sun to rule over the day, for his steadfast love endures forever;

9   the moon and stars to rule over the night, for his steadfast love endures forever;

10   to him who struck down the firstborn of Egypt, for his steadfast love endures forever;

11   and brought Israel out from among them, for his steadfast love endures forever;

12   with a strong hand and an outstretched arm, for his steadfast love endures forever;

13   to him who divided the Red Sea in two, for his steadfast love endures forever;

14   and made Israel pass through the midst of it, for his steadfast love endures forever;

# STEADFAST LOVE

We worship You today for who You are—God of gods and Lord of lords. Your goodness is supreme, and Your pure love is absolute, eternal.

We worship You today for the universe You created; You are the only source of all life. You did not create it and set it in motion only to ignore it. Your love blazes with every sunrise and beams from every full moon gleaming in the black velvet of night. Every minute, the world resonates with the wonders of Your love.

We worship You today for the deliverance You supply. In ages past, You delivered the Israelites from Egypt; now, through the sacrifice of Jesus, You deliver sinners from the gates of hell. Your wondrous love delivers us into Your eternal rest.

We worship You today for defeating our enemies by Your suffering on the cross. Israel warred against human enemies, and You gave that nation victory. We fight against spiritual enemies who would steal from us our inheritance, but Your fierce love protects us from our foes.

Yes, we worship You today for Your daily care of us. Your steadfast love sees that we are fed and clothed and rejoice in the pleasure of being alive. We thank You, God of heaven, that Your steadfast love endures forever.

15   but overthrew Pharaoh and his host in the Red Sea, for his steadfast love endures forever;

16   to him who led his people through the wilderness, for his steadfast love endures forever;

17   to him who struck down great kings, for his steadfast love endures forever;

18   and killed mighty kings, for his steadfast love endures forever;

19   Sihon, king of the Amorites, for his steadfast love endures forever;

20   and Og, king of Bashan, for his steadfast love endures forever;

21   and gave their land as a heritage, for his steadfast love endures forever;

22   a heritage to Israel his servant, for his steadfast love endures forever.

23   It is he who remembered us in our low estate, for his steadfast love endures forever;

24   and rescued us from our foes, for his steadfast love endures forever;

25   he who gives food to all flesh, for his steadfast love endures forever.

26   Give thanks to the God of heaven, for his steadfast love endures forever.

# My Prayer

_____

_____

_____

_____

_____

_____

_____

_____

_____

_____

_____

_____

_____

_____

_____

_____

_____

_____

_____

_____

_____

_____

# Psalm 137

1. By the waters of Babylon, there we sat down and wept, when we remembered Zion.

2. On the willows there we hung up our lyres.

3. For there our captors required of us songs, and our tormentors, mirth, saying, "Sing us one of the songs of Zion!"

4. How shall we sing the Lord's song in a foreign land?

5. If I forget you, O Jerusalem, let my right hand forget its skill!

6. Let my tongue stick to the roof of my mouth, if I do not remember you, if I do not set Jerusalem above my highest joy!

7. Remember, O Lord, against the Edomites the day of Jerusalem, how they said, "Lay it bare, lay it bare, down to its foundations!"

8. O daughter of Babylon, doomed to be destroyed, blessed shall he be who repays you with what you have done to us!

9. Blessed shall he be who takes your little ones and dashes them against the rock!

# MISSING THE SONG

Lord, I am in a dry and arid land. Because of my stubborn pride and my rebellion against Your commands, You expelled me to this place. My own thoughts taunt me: *Sing the songs of joy in the Lord. See what peace they bring You now.* My heart condemns me: *You are worse than that callow son who squandered his inheritance on parties and fast living. He was young and thoughtless, but you have no excuse. You refused to obey God's call to service, fleeing in your own direction.*

My heart is right to condemn me, Lord. Your instructions angered me. When I ran from You, I acted like a sulking child. Like a child, I find no satisfaction in this new place because I miss You. Here, I entertain people who speak Your Name only as a curse. I sing new songs beside streams of polluted water, and the songs themselves are polluted. My fingers stumble through the chords. My throat closes while I stutter through the lyrics. It's time to shed this too-tight life, hang up my lyre, and leave this place.

Lord, can I come home? Will You accept me? Can You ever love and trust me again? I'm sorry. I was wrong. I really did not know what was best for me. I repent for rejecting Your way. Please destroy my pride, kill my rebellion, and restore to me the joy of my salvation. Allow me once again to sing the song of the Lord.

# Psalm 138

1     I give you thanks, O Lord, with my whole heart; before the gods I sing your praise;

2     I bow down toward your holy temple and give thanks to your name for your steadfast love and your faithfulness, for you have exalted above all things your name and your word.

3     On the day I called, you answered me; my strength of soul you increased.

4     All the kings of the earth shall give you thanks, O Lord, for they have heard the words of your mouth,

5     and they shall sing of the ways of the Lord, for great is the glory of the Lord.

6     For though the Lord is high, he regards the lowly, but the haughty he knows from afar.

7     Though I walk in the midst of trouble, you preserve my life; you stretch out your hand against the wrath of my enemies, and your right hand delivers me.

8     The Lord will fulfill his purpose for me; your steadfast love, O Lord, endures forever. Do not forsake the work of your hands.

# WHAT WONDROUS LOVE!

My heart sings in praise of You, my Lord. In the presence of angels and saints, my heart overflows with gratitude. You adopted me into Your family, gave me Your Name, and set Your living Word in my soul. What wondrous love this is! You, who exalted Your Name and Your Word above all things in heaven and on earth, also placed them in this body of clay and put eternity in my heart.

How can it be that You, who created everything, take such a loving interest in this single, fragile part of Your creation? How amazing is Your loving care of me! I marvel at the way You meet my most trivial of needs—a parking spot in a crowded lot, a friend's touch in my loneliness. When I call on You, the eternal, holy One, You always answer me. The intimate time we spend together infuses my body and soul with strength. Because of Your love, I cherish every moment and delight in each day.

You make life so worth living that my heart's greatest desire is to see everyone from pauper to king know You as Lord and Savior. You deserve to hear all the kings on earth praise Your Name. Open their ears so they can hear You calling them to desert their pride and to follow You. Lord, by Your power and according to Your will, bring all the inhabitants of earth to sing of Your great glory. Great is the glory of our eternal King!

# Psalm 139

1     O Lord, you have searched me and known me!

2     You know when I sit down and when I rise up; you discern my thoughts from afar.

3     You search out my path and my lying down and are acquainted with all my ways.

4     Even before a word is on my tongue, behold, O Lord, you know it altogether.

5     You hem me in, behind and before, and lay your hand upon me.

6     Such knowledge is too wonderful for me; it is high; I cannot attain it.

7     Where shall I go from your Spirit? Or where shall I flee from your presence?

8     If I ascend to heaven, you are there! If I make my bed in Sheol, you are there!

9     If I take the wings of the morning and dwell in the uttermost parts of the sea,

10     even there your hand shall lead me, and your right hand shall hold me.

11     If I say, "Surely the darkness shall cover me, and the light about me be night,"

12     even the darkness is not dark to you; the night is bright as the day, for darkness is as light with you.

13     For you formed my inward parts; you knitted me together in my mother's womb.

# THE KNOWING

Father, Your ways are such a mystery to me. Your Spirit knows me intimately. He searched out all my ways as You created me. Your Spirit watches over me by night and cares for me by day. My plans lay spread out before You, and You see to the ends of my paths. I never surprise You. You already know my heart's impulses before they take the shape of words on my lips. You are a hedge surrounding me, protecting me from destruction. Your hand on my shoulder guides me safely past obstacles.

Why, Lord? Why do You care about me? It would be like me building a snowman, placing him in the shade, and carefully keeping the snow packed around him. If I had the ability to make the snowman aware of my work, would I do it? Would I care enough to give him an awareness of himself and of me?

Why, Lord, why? You are the eternal One. My life is like a single snowflake melting on a fingertip—exquisite beauty quickly gone. Why give me an awareness of You?

But that's what You have done, Lord. In the hurry and bustle of my day, in the back of my mind, Your presence ripples through my thoughts. You make my lowliest duties like a taste of heaven. When I fall on my bed in exhausted sleep, You protect me even in my dreams. I travel east and see You in a child's shy smile; I fly west and see Your glory in a many-colored sunset. If I fall into the pit of depression, You are there to comfort me and lift me out.

When You were creating me in my mother's womb, You knit together my soul and body. You shaped me in secret, safe and secure within my mother. You wove my substance into a living story whose end You knew before You set the beginning in motion. The precious thread You weave through my every day is the *knowing* that You are with me.

I have no words distinct enough or sentences clear enough to express my gratitude for Your giving me an awareness of You. You could work always in the background and my ignorance of You would be no hindrance to Your plans. Instead, You tell me Your thoughts and include me in Your purposes.

14   I praise you, for I am fearfully and wonderfully made. Wonderful are your works; my soul knows it very well.

15   My frame was not hidden from you, when I was being made in secret, intricately woven in the depths of the earth.

16   Your eyes saw my unformed substance; in your book were written, every one of them, the days that were formed for me, when as yet there were none of them.

17   How precious to me are your thoughts, O God! How vast is the sum of them!

18   If I would count them, they are more than the sand. I awake, and I am still with you.

19   Oh that you would slay the wicked, O God! O men of blood, depart from me!

20   They speak against you with malicious intent; your enemies take your name in vain!

21   Do I not hate those who hate you, O Lord? And do I not loathe those who rise up against you?

22   I hate them with complete hatred; I count them my enemies.

23   Search me, O God, and know my heart! Try me and know my thoughts!

24   And see if there be any grievous way in me, and lead me in the way everlasting!

Use me, Lord, to confront Your enemies. Let my life radiate Your glory and my lips speak Your offer of forgiveness to murderers, of redemption to liars, of love to haters, and of mercy for those who rise up against You. Could I do less when You have graciously given me all?

Father, root out the sin I cannot see in myself. Spirit of God, use every event in my life to refine and purify me. Continue to lead me in the everlasting way, where I will always be with You, where I will always be knowing You better.

# PSALM 140

1    Deliver me, O Lord, from evil men; preserve me from violent men,

2    who plan evil things in their heart and stir up wars continually.

3    They make their tongue sharp as a serpent's, and under their lips is the venom of asps.

*Selah*

4    Guard me, O Lord, from the hands of the wicked; preserve me from violent men, who have planned to trip up my feet.

5    The arrogant have hidden a trap for me, and with cords they have spread a net; beside the way they have set snares for me.

*Selah*

6    I say to the Lord, You are my God; give ear to the voice of my pleas for mercy, O Lord!

7    O Lord, my Lord, the strength of my salvation, you have covered my head in the day of battle.

8    Grant not, O Lord, the desires of the wicked; do not further their evil plot or they will be exalted!

*Selah*

9    As for the head of those who surround me, let the mischief of their lips overwhelm them!

10    Let burning coals fall upon them! Let them be cast into fire, into miry pits, no more to rise!

11    Let not the slanderer be established in the land; let evil hunt down the violent man speedily!

12    I know that the Lord will maintain the cause of the afflicted, and will execute justice for the needy.

13    Surely the righteous shall give thanks to your name; the upright shall dwell in your presence.

# Expose My Enemies

Father, I know it. I see it in Your Word, but I am defenseless against those who oppose me. My passion is to love and obey You. It seldom occurs to me that those around me may not share my goals or may not want to see Your kingdom come on earth. I assume that everyone else shares my desire to honor You, so I am surprised and shocked when I discover that someone I know is my enemy.

Thank You, Lord, that most of the people in my life do love You; these devoted friends come to my defense. However, they cannot deliver me from my enemies. Only You can do that; only You can preserve me. Please God, show Your power to my enemies as You protect me.

Convict those who think evil and speak poison. Confuse their thinking and confound their lies. When their talk becomes slander, show everyone that nothing they say is true. Crush their pride and transform it into humility; draw their eyes to You for salvation and forgiveness.

For my enemies who work in secret, behind my back, make their traps fall apart and cause their snares to close on emptiness. Show them that You see their treachery. Let them fall into their own traps so they will see their sins and turn to You in repentance.

Some of my enemies declare war. No slander or snares set in secret for them! They are confident they will defeat me. They trust in themselves, but I trust in You. You are my armor protecting even my thoughts on the day of battle. Defeat my enemies for Your Name's sake. Show them Your glory so they will confess Your excellence and exalt only You. Then all Your servants will praise You, and all Your enemies will bow before You. Together, we will proclaim You as Lord of all.

# PSALM 141

1   O Lord, I call upon you; hasten to me! Give ear to my voice when I call to you!

2   Let my prayer be counted as incense before you, and the lifting up of my hands as the evening sacrifice!

3   Set a guard, O Lord, over my mouth; keep watch over the door of my lips!

4   Do not let my heart incline to any evil, to busy myself with wicked deeds in company with men who work iniquity, and let me not eat of their delicacies!

5   Let a righteous man strike me—it is a kindness; let him rebuke me—it is oil for my head; let my head not refuse it. Yet my prayer is continually against their evil deeds.

6   When their judges are thrown over the cliff, then they shall hear my words, for they are pleasant.

7   As when one plows and breaks up the earth, so shall our bones be scattered at the mouth of Sheol.

8   But my eyes are toward you, O God, my Lord; in you I seek refuge; leave me not defenseless!

9   Keep me from the trap that they have laid for me and from the snares of evildoers!

10  Let the wicked fall into their own nets, while I pass by safely.

# BEST FRIEND

Lord, I'm in a hurry and really need Your help. I have this new friend. Everyone admires her because she's pretty and always wears the latest styles. I don't know why she chose me to be her friend. I feel self-conscious around her and I don't know what to say.

Should I become friends with her, Lord? What does she want? If we become best friends, will she draw me away from You, or will we help each other know You better? Will she tempt me to go places or to do things that would shame me before You?

I'm confused, Lord. Before I spend more time with her, lead me to someone who knows her well. Help me learn the good and the bad, her strengths and her weaknesses. Give me courage to ask my new friend what she thinks about You. Guide me to make a good decision about sharing my life with her.

Lord, if this new friendship is an opportunity from You, I will delight in getting to know her better. You know how lonely I've been. It would be wonderful to have a best friend.

However, Lord, if this relationship is a temptation to replace You as the most important one in my life, please guide me safely past this trap. Protect me from the pain of discovering that she was a false friend and only wanted to use me. Strengthen me to keep my eyes on You because I love You best. You are my best friend forever.

# Psalm 142

1    With my voice I cry out to the Lord; with my voice I plead for mercy to the Lord.

2    I pour out my complaint before him; I tell my trouble before him.

3    When my spirit faints within me, you know my way! In the path where I walk they have hidden a trap for me.

4    Look to the right and see: there is none who takes notice of me; no refuge remains to me; no one cares for my soul.

5    I cry to you, O Lord; I say, "You are my refuge, my portion in the land of the living."

6    Attend to my cry, for I am brought very low! Deliver me from my persecutors, for they are too strong for me!

7    Bring me out of prison, that I may give thanks to your name! The righteous will surround me, for you will deal bountifully with me.

# Pastor's Prayer

Look at me, Lord. You called me to pastor this church. I came with high hopes, and I anticipated great joy in seeing You work in this place. My desire was to see Your people in the congregation grow in every way. Shortly after I arrived, however, I learned this flock of docile sheep was actually a collection of irritated cats. Not one followed willingly, and each was confident he or she knew what You wanted us to do next—and every plan was different!

What am I to do? My knees have buckled under the weight of this load. I have landed on my face before Your throne.

I feel like Elijah felt when he ran away from Jezebel and wanted to die. He thought he was the only person left in Israel who followed You. That's the way I feel, Lord. Look around me. Do You see anyone from the church who cares about the condition of my life? Who are the people praying for me? Where are the fellow workers, like Elisha for Elijah and Barnabas for Paul, to assist me in this work? All I can see are certain members of the congregation attempting to manipulate me for their own purposes.

Can You see just how desperate I am? I've tried standing up to the deacons; I want to be faithful to the vision You've given me. This congregation has the potential to be a vibrant, healthy, mature church family that serves You, their families, and our community. But every time I propose something different, they block it.

I am so weary, Lord. I want to resign from the church, crawl off somewhere to heal, and be something besides a pastor.

There, I've said it, Lord, words I thought I would never say. I am tired beyond expressing, lying captive in this prison of my soul. You are my only hope. I no longer have the strength to forge ahead, no power to lead this congregation. I've been knocked down too many times.

You are my only hope. Only You can lift me from this deep depression and shift this overwhelming burden from my soul. Only You know the whole story.

# My Prayer

_____

_____

_____

_____

_____

_____

_____

_____

_____

_____

_____

_____

_____

_____

_____

_____

_____

_____

You are my foundation—the bedrock of my life—the only thing that remains at this moment. Heal me, Father; just as You sent angels and birds to meet Elijah's needs, come to me, speak peace to me, and let me rest in Your arms. Cover me with Your feathers and hide me under Your wings while You restore my soul.

# Psalm 143

1     Hear my prayer, O Lord; give ear to my pleas for mercy! In your faithfulness answer me, in your righteousness!

2     Enter not into judgment with your servant, for no one living is righteous before you.

3     For the enemy has pursued my soul; he has crushed my life to the ground; he has made me sit in darkness like those long dead.

4     Therefore my spirit faints within me; my heart within me is appalled.

5     I remember the days of old; I meditate on all that you have done; I ponder the work of your hands.

6     I stretch out my hands to you; my soul thirsts for you like a parched land.

*Selah*

7     Answer me quickly, O Lord! My spirit fails! Hide not your face from me, lest I be like those who go down to the pit.

8     Let me hear in the morning of your steadfast love, for in you I trust. Make me know the way I should go, for to you I lift up my soul.

9     Deliver me from my enemies, O Lord! I have fled to you for refuge!

10     Teach me to do your will, for you are my God! Let your good Spirit lead me on level ground!

11     For your name's sake, O Lord, preserve my life! In your righteousness bring my soul out of trouble!

12     And in your steadfast love you will cut off my enemies, and you will destroy all the adversaries of my soul, for I am your servant.

# The Crossroads

I am weary, Lord. The battle has been fierce. In the confusion of the fight, I have lost my way. I acted without considering the consequences. I found myself surrounded by my enemies. When I tried to flee, they wounded me, leaving me with a fainting spirit and a desolate heart.

I failed You, Lord. Your Spirit convicts me of my sin. Have mercy on me. I boldly claim Your forgiveness because of Your faithfulness in previous days. I stood condemned for my sins on the day You invited me to accept Your gift of forgiveness, of salvation. Oh, the memory of the freedom I felt that day—forgiven, cleansed, and adopted into Your family.

The joy, strength, and sense of purpose I discovered that day no longer fuel my life. Thank You that You are faithful to never let me go, but my soul thirsts to know again the joy of my salvation.

I stand at a crossroads, Father. I consider, undecided, fearing to travel a path that will lead me further from You. My spirit quakes before the decision I must make. Even if You speak to me, will I hear You? Don't hide Your face from me, Lord. Shine clear light, like the light of the rising sun, on the road I should choose. My desire is to follow Your path if only Your Spirit will guide me.

Yes, I want to serve You with an undivided heart once more. Strengthen me in Your love, and set me back on my feet, ready to battle the enemies of my soul until You destroy them. Only You can preserve my life.

# Psalm 144

1   Blessed be the Lord, my rock, who trains my hands for war, and my fingers for battle;

2   he is my steadfast love and my fortress, my stronghold and my deliverer, my shield and he in whom I take refuge, who subdues peoples under me.

3   O Lord, what is man that you regard him, or the son of man that you think of him?

4   Man is like a breath; his days are like a passing shadow.

5   Bow your heavens, O Lord, and come down! Touch the mountains so that they smoke!

6   Flash forth the lightning and scatter them; send out your arrows and rout them!

7   Stretch out your hand from on high; rescue me and deliver me from the many waters, from the hand of foreigners,

8   whose mouths speak lies and whose right hand is a right hand of falsehood.

9   I will sing a new song to you, O God; upon a ten-stringed harp I will play to you,

10  who gives victory to kings, who rescues David his servant from the cruel sword.

11  Rescue me and deliver me from the hand of foreigners, whose mouths speak lies and whose right hand is a right hand of falsehood.

12  May our sons in their youth be like plants full grown, our daughters like corner pillars cut for the structure of a palace;

# ONE SOLDIER AT WAR

Almighty God, You recruited me into Your army. You trained me with Your weapons of warfare. You taught me to trust You to shield me from the tempter's arrows. You showed me how to use the sword of Your Word to confound the propaganda slipped in through my old, sinful nature. You tutored me in prayer to intercede for those who perish in the enemy's prison camps. You taught me to fight against the spiritual enemies of my soul.

As Your soldier, I am always on call, ready for duty. Nevertheless, I fail to understand *why* You want me to serve in Your army. Every word You speak is more powerful than the greatest explosive. Legions of angels await Your orders, but my life is like a flickering candle; I have no power in myself. My days are just puffs of breath on a cold morning; even so, You use me to battle the tide of evil that seeks like a tsunami to wash us away.

I am a grain of sand against this flood, but You are mighty. Come down from on high to strike those who seek to deceive me with their handclasps of false peace. Stretch out Your hand and rescue me from the ones who want to destroy me with their lies. Protect me, Lord, from those who declare that You are not God and demand I worship another.

Thank You, Lord, for Your presence in my heart, assuring me that the war has been won and that these battles are only to mop up the enemy. You will soon reveal Yourself as the ruler of all nations, and complete peace will come. In that time, all our children will grow in strength and beauty, our lives will be prosperous, and fear will find no place in our hearts. Blessings without number will be our delight. We will sing a mighty song of deliverance in Your presence, and that will be worth fighting any battle.

**13**     may our granaries be full, providing all kinds of produce; may our sheep bring forth thousands and ten thousands in our fields;

**14**     may our cattle be heavy with young, suffering no mishap or failure in bearing; may there be no cry of distress in our streets!

**15**     Blessed are the people to whom such blessings fall! Blessed are the people whose God is the Lord!

# My Prayer

_____

_____

_____

_____

_____

_____

_____

_____

_____

_____

_____

_____

_____

_____

_____

_____

_____

_____

_____

_____

_____

_____

# Psalm 145

1   I will extol you, my God and King, and bless your name forever and ever.

2   Every day I will bless you and praise your name forever and ever.

3   Great is the Lord, and greatly to be praised, and his greatness is unsearchable.

4   One generation shall commend your works to another, and shall declare your mighty acts.

5   On the glorious splendor of your majesty, and on your wondrous works, I will meditate.

6   They shall speak of the might of your awesome deeds, and I will declare your greatness.

7   They shall pour forth the fame of your abundant goodness and shall sing aloud of your righteousness.

8   The Lord is gracious and merciful, slow to anger and abounding in steadfast love.

9   The Lord is good to all, and his mercy is over all that he has made.

10  All your works shall give thanks to you, O Lord, and all your saints shall bless you!

11  They shall speak of the glory of your kingdom and tell of your power,

12  to make known to the children of man your mighty deeds, and the glorious splendor of your kingdom.

13  Your kingdom is an everlasting kingdom, and your dominion endures throughout all generations. The Lord is faithful in all his words and kind in all his works.

# MY FOREVER KING

Eternal One, my forever King, my heart overflows with wonder and amazement. I fall on my knees and bow before You. You called *me* into Your eternal kingdom. I never tire of thanking You for saving me. You restored me to the place You prepared for me. You made me a citizen in Your glorious kingdom.

Oh, wonderful thought: Your kingdom is eternal, so my new life in Christ gives me forever to search out the unknowable heights and the unfathomable depths of Your greatness. But why should I wait until I reach heaven to begin my search? I will start now and continue when I reach my new home, where the smog of sin will no longer cloud my sight of You.

The idols of man-made gods come and go, but not one can replace You. No ruler can wipe the knowledge of You from the pages of human history. Those who worship You always tell their families of Your mighty works, so I too will continue that legacy and declare Your greatness every day.

You are genuinely patient, giving every person time to turn to You in repentance. Your every small blessing and Your powerful, miraculous works display Your grace and mercy. They foretell of the glorious splendor of Your kingdom.

You raise up those who bow down before You and confess that You are King of all. You satisfy the needs of those who depend on You. You are holy and always kind, and You save us when we call out to You in distress. My mouth will always have reasons to praise You, God. Forever and ever, I will declare the worthiness of my forever King.

14 The Lord upholds all who are falling and raises up all who are bowed down.

15 The eyes of all look to you, and you give them their food in due season.

16 You open your hand; you satisfy the desire of every living thing.

17 The Lord is righteous in all his ways and kind in all his works.

18 The Lord is near to all who call on him, to all who call on him in truth.

19 He fulfills the desire of those who fear him; he also hears their cry and saves them.

20 The Lord preserves all who love him, but all the wicked he will destroy.

21 My mouth will speak the praise of the Lord, and let all flesh bless his holy name forever and ever.

# My Prayer

_____

_____

_____

_____

_____

_____

_____

_____

_____

_____

_____

_____

_____

_____

_____

_____

_____

_____

_____

_____

_____

_____

# Psalm 146

1   Praise the Lord! Praise the Lord, O my soul!

2   I will praise the Lord as long as I live; I will sing praises to my God while I have my being.

3   Put not your trust in princes, in a son of man, in whom there is no salvation.

4   When his breath departs he returns to the earth; on that very day his plans perish.

5   Blessed is he whose help is the God of Jacob, whose hope is in the Lord his God,

6   who made heaven and earth, the sea, and all that is in them, who keeps faith forever;

7   who executes justice for the oppressed, who gives food to the hungry. The Lord sets the prisoners free;

8   the Lord opens the eyes of the blind. The Lord lifts up those who are bowed down; the Lord loves the righteous.

9   The Lord watches over the sojourners; he upholds the widow and the fatherless, but the way of the wicked he brings to ruin.

10  The Lord will reign forever, your God, O Zion, to all generations. Praise the Lord!

# FAR FROM FUTILE

You know, Lord, I feel sorry for King Solomon sometimes. He declared, after living his life in search of meaning, that everything under the sun was useless activity. He found that every plan of man ended in futility because death put an end to those who had planned. But what good was his wisdom when he missed one of the most important of Your secrets?

Father, Your Word shows clearly that it's not *our* plans that matter; it's *Yours* that matter. When I consent to depend on You instead of myself, my world changes. My plans to become as powerful as possible no longer motivate me. Instead, I pursue justice for the oppressed. I drop my plans to hoard large quantities of wealth and look for ways to feed the hungry. I work to free prisoners from addiction, pride, and selfishness. I pray that the blind will discover their need for Your forgiveness when You open their eyes. I am Your hands and feet as I care for strangers, widows, and the fatherless. I am Your heart as I love Your children and encourage them to follow You.

Just as Solomon said, my plans are futile, but Your plans are far from futile. None of the work done in Your Name and by Your Spirit is done in vain. Every drop of cold water, each tenderly spoken word ripples through this world and rolls across the oceans of time to wash upon the shores of eternity, where they sparkle like gems in the light of the Son.

I praise You, Lord, for giving me a life worth living. I find not Solomon's "vanity of vanities" because I know that the blessings of my earthly life—lived Your way—last forever.

# Psalm 147

---

1   Praise the Lord! For it is good to sing praises to our God; for it is pleasant, and a song of praise is fitting.

2   The Lord builds up Jerusalem; he gathers the outcasts of Israel.

3   He heals the brokenhearted and binds up their wounds.

4   He determines the number of the stars; he gives to all of them their names.

5   Great is our Lord, and abundant in power; his understanding is beyond measure.

6   The Lord lifts up the humble; he casts the wicked to the ground.

7   Sing to the Lord with thanksgiving; make melody to our God on the lyre!

8   He covers the heavens with clouds; he prepares rain for the earth; he makes grass grow on the hills.

9   He gives to the beasts their food, and to the young ravens that cry.

10  His delight is not in the strength of the horse, nor his pleasure in the legs of a man,

11  but the Lord takes pleasure in those who fear him, in those who hope in his steadfast love.

12  Praise the Lord, O Jerusalem! Praise your God, O Zion!

13  For he strengthens the bars of your gates; he blesses your children within you.

14  He makes peace in your borders; he fills you with the finest of the wheat.

15  He sends out his command to the earth; his word runs swiftly.

# LOST AMONG THE MOUNTAINS

Lord, I sing Your praises today even though it is not an easy day for me to do so. All I can see are towering mountains of problems, uncertainties, and failures, and the vertical cliffs freeze me in fear. It seems that a single step in any direction will cause me to tumble into a chasm of defeat. Since I cannot find a safe step to take, I will stand and praise You.

My home is in shambles, just as Jerusalem was when it was destroyed by its enemies. You restored Jerusalem, and You can reestablish my home as well. That's almost too easy for You, God—the One who creates, the namer of every star. You are abundant in power and wise beyond measure.

My soul languishes in a high desert. My close companionship with You seems a distant dream. Nevertheless, I sing praises of thanksgiving. You, my God, the God who waters the earth with rain, snow, and hail in their seasons, will not leave my soul in a dry, desolate place. You delight in me as I hope in Your steadfast love even when You seem hidden to me.

My relationships with my family are frozen in anger, discontent, and conflict. I praise You for promising to bless my children, to make peace between family members, and to provide for every need. You, who commands the weather and sends a warm breeze at the perfect moment, can just as easily thaw hearts and heal the brokenhearted in my family.

I have not moved; none of my problems or circumstances has changed. Even so, Lord, You have reduced my mountains to molehills by declaring Your Word in my heart and changing my attitude. I will stand, watch You work, and trust You. Since I cannot find a safe step to take, I will stand and praise You. I will always praise You, Lord.

16    He gives snow like wool; he scatters hoarfrost like ashes.

17    He hurls down his crystals of ice like crumbs; who can stand before his cold?

18    He sends out his word, and melts them; he makes his wind blow and the waters flow.

19    He declares his word to Jacob, his statutes and rules to Israel.

20    He has not dealt thus with any other nation; they do not know his rules. Praise the Lord!

# My Prayer

_____

_____

_____

_____

_____

_____

_____

_____

_____

_____

_____

_____

_____

_____

_____

_____

_____

_____

_____

_____

_____

_____

# Psalm 148

1    Praise the Lord! Praise the Lord from the heavens; praise him in the heights!

2    Praise him, all his angels; praise him, all his hosts!

3    Praise him, sun and moon, praise him, all you shining stars!

4    Praise him, you highest heavens, and you waters above the heavens!

5    Let them praise the name of the Lord! For he commanded and they were created.

6    And he established them forever and ever; he gave a decree, and it shall not pass away.

7    Praise the Lord from the earth, you great sea creatures and all deeps,

8    fire and hail, snow and mist, stormy wind fulfilling his word!

9    Mountains and all hills, fruit trees and all cedars!

10    Beasts and all livestock, creeping things and flying birds!

11    Kings of the earth and all peoples, princes and all rulers of the earth!

12    Young men and maidens together, old men and children!

13    Let them praise the name of the Lord, for his name alone is exalted; his majesty is above earth and heaven.

14    He has raised up a horn for his people, praise for all his saints, for the people of Israel who are near to him. Praise the Lord!

# Now Is the Day to Praise

Today is the perfect day to praise You, Lord. Souls are awakening in Your kingdom; they have been born spiritually through the sacrifice of Jesus in the power of Your Spirit. Angels and all the heavenly hosts rejoice in these new births. They congratulate You on restoring these rebels to their rightful inheritance. All heaven celebrates and praises You, eternal One.

All creation praises You, from the waters above the highest heavens to those in the ocean depths. Creatures wild and tame praise Your Name. Weather is the language of the air as it sings Your praises. Mountaintops and gently rolling hills proclaim Your praise. Fruit trees and wildflowers display Your praise in every blossom. Every element of creation praises You now, today, this moment, forever.

When all the rest of creation praises You, oh Lord, will people not praise You? The children of Your kingdom praise You. I will praise You as I speak encouragement to others: "Kings, princes, and all rulers, praise the Name of the Lord. Young men and maidens, remember that Yahweh alone is exalted. Old men and children, regard God's majesty on the earth and in the heavens."

Your children will praise You now and forever. Those who turn their backs on Your love do not praise You now, but on the day of the Lord, they will bow in praise of You. Even as eternity fades away, those who love You will continually find more reasons to praise You.

# Psalm 149

1  Praise the Lord! Sing to the Lord a new song, his praise in the assembly of the godly!

2  Let Israel be glad in his Maker; let the children of Zion rejoice in their King!

3  Let them praise his name with dancing, making melody to him with tambourine and lyre!

4  For the Lord takes pleasure in his people; he adorns the humble with salvation.

5  Let the godly exult in glory; let them sing for joy on their beds.

6  Let the high praises of God be in their throats and two-edged swords in their hands,

7  to execute vengeance on the nations and punishments on the peoples,

8  to bind their kings with chains and their nobles with fetters of iron,

9  to execute on them the judgment written! This is honor for all his godly ones. Praise the Lord!

# THE BRIDE'S SONG

Praise the Lord!

What a wondrous day to praise You, Lord! We sing a song of salvation; we sing of Your perfect beauty, Jesus, and of the brilliance of the kingdom. You created it by Your death on the cross. Your resurrection brought us to it in new life. You have done it all.

The great day is here. The fullness of time has arrived. The number of believers is complete. Your church, Your bride, is ready. We praise You, Lord, for it is the time of Your return for Your bride. We stand in Your holiness, clothed in purest white, adorned in the salvation of our King. Ready to rise with praise and rejoicing, we come out at the blast of Your trumpet. We dance with delight and sing the bride's song of love. Never has such a joyous sound of praise been heard.

The whole world vibrates in celebration, Lord. The song fills the air surrounding the earth. Everything with ears hears the love song the bride sings to You. For some, the song reveals another opportunity to humbly cry out for forgiveness.

Nevertheless, the sound of the song is a two-edged sword. Many people shriek in terror, hiss in anger, or turn away in pride. On these, You pronounce judgment and write the document sealing their sentence. You give Your godly ones the honor of executing judgment on Your enemies. We will rule by Your side forever, loving You always with our hearts, our lives, and our songs.

We praise You, Lord.

# Psalm 150

1    Praise the Lord! Praise God in his sanctuary; praise him in his mighty heavens!

2    Praise him for his mighty deeds; praise him according to his excellent greatness!

3    Praise him with trumpet sound; praise him with lute and harp!

4    Praise him with tambourine and dance; praise him with strings and pipe!

5    Praise him with sounding cymbals; praise him with loud clashing cymbals!

6    Let everything that has breath praise the Lord! Praise the Lord!

# Eternal Delight

We come to You, eternal God, in a festival of joy. We attend You in Your sanctuary and celebrate You in our love and our delight. Command all the hosts of the highest heavens to join us in our praise, for we are too few to give You the praise and worship You deserve.

We praise You for Your mighty deeds, for You conquered death and set the captives free. We praise You, holy and exalted One, for You are the pure and righteous judge. You expose the lies of evil; You reveal Yourself as the way, the truth, and the life.

Our voices alone are not enough to express our delight in worshipping You. We add the joyous sounds of every type of musical instrument— brass, woodwinds, strings, and percussion. We dance with abandon before You, Lord. Now we are fully, completely alive and join with all creation to celebrate Your glory, to praise You, and to worship You for all eternity.

Praise the Lord!